Unfolding Further

More World Travels on a Folding Bike

GIANNI FILIPPINI

COPYRIGHT © 2023 BY GIANNI FILIPPINI

ALL RIGHTS RESERVED.

THIS BOOK OR ANY PORTION THEREOF
MAY NOT BE REPRODUCED OR USED IN ANY MANNER
WHATSOEVER WITHOUT THE EXPRESS WRITTEN
PERMISSION OF THE AUTHOR EXCEPT FOR THE
USE OF BRIEF QUOTATIONS IN A BOOK REVIEW.

FIRST PRINTING EDITION, 2023

ISBN 9798869687241

DRAWINGS BY GIANNI FILIPPINI

IN GRATITUDE TO SIMON STOTT FOR
CORRECTING THE ORIGINAL MANUSCRIPT

WWW.BROMPTONTRAVELER.COM

* * *

Table of Contents

Introduction 1

Carretera Austral 7

Long Way Home 27

Southern England 53

Scottish Highlands 73

Sicily's South 93

Northern Med 111

Portugal's Coast 131

Turkish Delight 147

Colombian Andes 179

Across Hokkaido 203

Unfolding Further

1. CARRETERA AUSTRAL
2. LONG WAY HOME
3. SOUTHERN ENGLAND
4. SCOTTISH HIGHLANDS
5. SICILY'S SOUTH
6. NORTHERN MED
7. PORTUGAL'S COAST
8. TURKISH DELIGHT
9. COLOMBIAN ANDES
10. ACROSS HOKKAIDO

Introduction

'Traveling is a brutality. It forces you to trust strangers and to lose sight of all the familiar comforts of home and friends. You are constantly off balance. Nothing is yours except the essential things. - air, sleep, dreams, the sea, the sky. - all things tending towards the eternal or what we imagine of it.'

- CESARE PAVESE -

The wide-eyed country boy who dreamt of embarking on thrilling adventures on two wheels has long blossomed into a fully-fledged adult, yet that same yearning to rediscover the mesmerising wonders of nature has gracefully stood the test of time, burning as bright as the first day it was kindled. That is not something to be taken for granted. I had just returned aching and limping from a bike trip in Pakistan, where an epic fall could not only have messed up my planned expedition but, more seriously, ended my life. Luckily I had recovered fully after a couple of months' rest, grateful it had not turned out to be worse. Unsettled by the whole experience, I was aware that it had taught me something and that next time I could be a little wiser. I also knew that I should not dwell on it too much, otherwise I risked being afraid of doing what I most enjoyed. I was soon eager to get back on a bicycle and started planning more rides as the best way to get over the experience. The next ride was scheduled to be in Patagonia and the road choice was none other than the Carretera Austral, a mythical road that for centuries has fascinated adventurers, cyclists, motorbikers, poets, revolutionaries, writers and bandits. I suppose I could have started with something less challenging but I wanted to rebuild the confidence and trust, that I know is the best antidote to the worrying thoughts and the what-ifs that can paralyse us and stop us from living our lives; it was time for a paradigm shift where everything has a meaning and nothing can really go wrong after all. As hinted by the book title, I was envisaging going "further" than I had been before, reaching far off corners I had not yet explored. As it turned out, life had a different plan and events took a surprising turn - and I, like everyone else, had to learn to cope with and navigate this. While in South America, about to cross the border between Chile and Argentina, the COVID-19 pandemic first appeared on the horizon. What had started as unworrying news bulletins turned more gruesome by the day and were soon filled with images of people clad in boiler suits and goggles and stories of lockdowns that seemed to have come out of a dystopian novel. In the freedom-loving world I live in, it was easy to discount those early reports as something that could only happen elsewhere. We all know how that went... Fortunately, unlike many travellers who ended up being stranded in far off places and left to deal with the extraordinary, I made it safely back to England just in time.

- Brutus -

Moreover, with air transport grinding to a halt, I suddenly found myself with much more time on my hands than I had ever had in my life. I thought I should make the most of it and use the limitations, to discover places that I had so far put off for a later time or even discounted. Over the years I had done some short tours in England, for example, but they were always limited to weekends in late spring or summer, when the forecasts were better than average. As for European countries, I had always thought I should leave them as part of my retirement plan when long haul travel might not be as easy and being closer to home would be a much safer option.

There is always a tendency to take what is within easy reach for granted. Even the most beautiful and compelling places become ordinary when they are too familiar and right on our doorstep. I know this well from experience. I was blessed to be born not far from the Dolomites, some of the most spectacular mountain landscapes on the planet. Yet they have always felt too close to home to be really appreciated and, as a result, I have often searched for that same beauty elsewhere. I had so far ignored much of England and the Old Continent. Biking through Europe of course is a remarkable experience; it combines breathtaking scenery, a rich history, and many diverse cultures. From the rugged peaks of the Alps to the sun-kissed beaches of the Mediterranean, Europe is also the cradle of cycling and home to some of the most iconic bike routes the world has to offer. Eurovelo routes, as I would later discover, were the result of many European-sponsored projects aimed at creating an extensive network of cycling routes that link countries across the Continent. With limitations on travel changing faster than clouds on a windy day, I discovered yet another advantage of cycling as a means of transport. As the virus spread with no mercy, there were times when strict rules made it impossible to cross into another country, whether on a plane, a train or by car on a highway. It was on one such occasion when, tempting fate a little, I succeeded in fulfilling a long held dream of cycling from England, my adopted country, to my birthplace across the

Italian Alps. Borders along those wonderful European cycling routes had long been forgotten and strict regulations and controls did not seem to apply to the niche of international long haul cyclists! What was a curse for most and a tragedy for some, felt at times a blessing. I had the unique opportunity to experience some of Europe's most enchanting destinations, charming towns and stunning landscapes at leisure and rediscover the simple pleasures of spending time connecting to nature and the outdoors.

Never before did such reconnection feel more timely and appropriate to me. Cycling in nature was the best healer at a time when physical and mental well-being had been put through a serious stress test. I had to get back to nature to feel more grounded, balanced, and connected to the world around me. Bike travel is more than just a way to see new places - it's also a mindset, a way of life and a great teacher. It taught me once again the importance of embracing uncertainty at a time when we were constantly asked to be cautious and it seemed natural to fight against it. I also learnt that, ultimately, whether one travels near or far is not that important; either way it is likely to enrich us with valuable experiences and unforgettable memories.

After years of faithful and reliable service I also felt it was time to replace Bronte, the old trusted bike that had accompanied me on the adventures detailed in 'Unfolding Travels'. It had served me well over the years and was still a good ride but it was inevitably a bit battered; foreseeing many more future journeys I put in an order for a new bike. Not surprisingly, it was much of the same with the exception of trading a pale green frame for a darker black one. It still looked like a small, endearing folding bike, but due to its sombre colour and for the sake of incongruity I thought I would call it Brutus. Brutus would turn out to be as reliable as Bronte and carried me along more wonderful journeys and spectacular roads in the most diverse of places from Scotland, to Sicily, to Colombia and the old bike-touring favourite that is Turkey. Whether you're a seasoned cyclist or a novice, I hope these cycling stories through Europe and elsewhere will inspire and empower you to plan your own future adventures and spark an interest in some new destinations. If the reader has already experienced the incredible rewards that await those who are brave enough to embrace such journeys, maybe there will also be a rekindling of emotions felt when pedalling along familiar routes or fond recollections of places once visited.

At the beginning of each chapter, you will discover a map illustrating the route taken. For those interested, at the end of every chapter I included a QR code that directly links to the video showcasing the relevant journey on my YouTube channel.

With gratitude.
Gianni

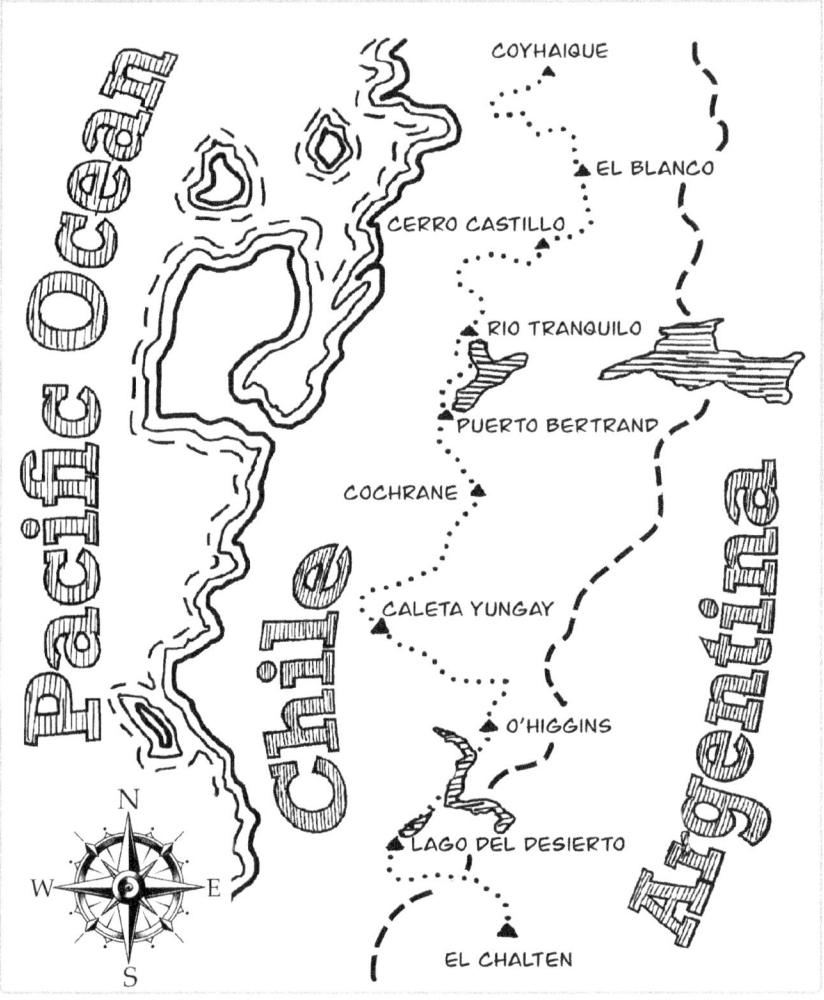

Carretera Austral

I completed the following journey just before a particularly nasty virus strain turned pandemic and wreaked havoc around the world, changing lots of people's plans. What persuaded me to visit South America, and Chile in particular, was a legendary road, Ruta 7, better known as Carretera Austral. Its construction was started in the seventies and the plan was to connect some of the most remote communities of Chilean Patagonia. Fifty years later, the complex task is still no more than work in progress, marred by the challenging features of the landscape, extreme weather conditions, landslides, glaciers and floods. It is still a mess of a road that repels car traffic as much as it attracts daring cyclists.

La Carretera cuts through the spine of Patagonia for over a thousand kilometres connecting Puerto Montt, the starting point in the north, to Villa O'Higgins down south. My trusted Bronte was recalled from an early retirement. Old and a little battered, it certainly didn't deserve further abuse; but I was left with no other choice due to a delay in receiving a new bike. I knew progress on this route would be slow and, in hindsight, wisely decided to shorten the length of the journey, cutting it in half. After an early morning flight from the capital Santiago to the airport of Balmaceda, I took a bus transfer to Coyhaique, the first and last proper town I would encounter on this Patagonian journey.

A little worn by the long journey, I thought I should start gently. The bike was quickly unpacked and assembled under the shining sun; I was ready to set off with a bang. Hardly had I started to pedal when, a few hundred meters beyond the town centre, I had a record breaking flat tyre. I also felt deflated, but counted to ten, determined to not swear. I pulled to a side verge and started to fiddle with the wheel. Eventually I found a tiny sharp piece of metal that was stuck in the tyre, which I must have carried all the way back from my previous trip to Pakistan. A couple of hours after this false start, I reached the tiny village of El Blanco, pushed by the most benevolent of tailwinds.

In the morning, Señora Maria produced a nice breakfast with freshly baked bread rolls and a glorious homemade gooseberry jam. These round berries could be picked by simply stretching an arm out of her kitchen window. I consumed my hefty meal while watching some gloomy television forecasts that didn't leave much hope. There was a unanimous hundred percent chance of rain. A quick glance outside the dining room window confirmed this. Clouds were hanging heavy, the colour of lead. I was expecting my fair share of wind and rain in Patagonia and it looked as if I wasn't going to be kept waiting. Two elderly Canadians cyclists, Bob and Rose, were also staying on the premises. I had met them the previous evening in the common kitchen area by the campsite; they were debating whether, after a long day cycling, they should get their dinner by going fishing for salmon in the local river. I have always been a great admirer of Canadians' outdoor skills. While I need shops for my food, just give them a knife, a fishing cane and a little pepper spray and they can happily live like the Flintstones. I began to climb up a soggy mountain.

The weatherman had not been precise. It only rained ninety percent of the time, but so much so that I felt miserable and soaked for most of the day. On top of the mountain pass it turned into a ruthless storm that had me taking refuge in one of the wooden huts of an empty campsite. It offered some respite, but I wasn't getting any drier and decided to move on to at least keep warm. Late afternoon, the clouds parted a little letting the timid sun pierce through. I had the first views of big mountains, still covered with patches of snow. Life in Patagonia can be rather harsh, a price one has to pay for the reward of a raw, unspoilt nature. I cycled for days through nothing but forests, lakes and rivers, but with very little food. Leaving Cerro Castillo, I spotted a farm and knew it could be my only chance of a hot breakfast. A man was standing at a distance by the entrance gate and I waved at him pointing at my mouth. He raised his hand high in a waiting signal and disappeared into the house. He soon re-emerged with a smile, the wife had granted the final permit. Eleuterio was his name. He welcomed me into the warm dining room and invited me to sit down while he raised the volume of an accordion playing a tango on the radio. His wife laid the table and brought me some boiled water, instant coffee powder, hot bread buns, margarine and a saucer filled to the brim with jam. I don't mean to be ungrateful, but had I come to this remote part of Chile for good food, I would have been sorely disappointed.

Herds of cattle happily grazing were a common sight along the road, yet my hopes for a good cup of white coffee were regularly dashed. Each time I asked for some milk I was presented with a large jar of powder. Similarly, chickens roamed freely in the garden, but when I asked for an omelette I was told to come back in a couple of weeks. Of course I don't blame them. Only these people know what it means to face the long Patagonian winters, and their generosity can stretch only so far for a cyclist passing by in the summer. I don't altogether trust my Spanish, but I think the wife explained that it was just a question of bad timing. There were new born chicks around and the hens were being given a little break, dashing all hopes for an omelette. Hanging from a metal hook in the kitchen I saw a shoulder of lamb, but it needed cooking; otherwise it was not worth carrying. I wasn't equipped with a gas stove and was limited to cold meals. I contemplated how different life might have been were I born a Canadian. My mind played with fantasies of a night camp where a log fire was burning and I could smell the scent of a glorious barbecue all around me. Eleuterio cheered me up by telling me that there were many mountain lions around.

"But you shouldn't worry." he said.

"There is plenty of game up in the mountains. I doubt they'd be interested in a skinny cyclist."

I thanked them for the warm breakfast and moved on with my journey. A few kilometres further on the Carretera Austral came to an abrupt halt, as if they had suddenly run out of tarmac. I moved down a single step and made my first acquaintance with 'el ripio', some nice sounding Spanish best translated as 'road under construction, opening date to be confirmed'. These are a common occurrence all over South America; failed efforts to link remote villages while extremely successful in wrecking cars. I rode on the loose rocks gently, using all my available gears, one to six and the emergency seventh which I call 'the walk'. I was slow, but made some progress. Given the bad conditions of the road and the unpredictable weather I had so far encountered, I was feeling a little hesitant about my endeavour. I gave myself a thirty percent chance of ever getting to the end.

The sun made the odd appearance through thick clouds, but I was still dealing with some rather unsettled weather. Past Cerro Castillo the road went through a rather remote and flat stretch, following the Ibanez river. It drizzled on and off most of the day and I ended up pitching my tent on a less than ideal spot. The following day I was in for a bit of a shock and a very busy morning. The evening before it had looked like an idyllic place to spend the night. It was a short walk away from the road, hidden on a rocky patch by a stream supplying fresh and pure drinking water. After I had set up my tent it started raining, so I congratulated myself on the good timing that ensured I would stay dry. At night it turned into a mighty storm that hurled down rain in buckets, lasting for the whole night. I woke up in the morning with a bouncy feel that made my inflatable mattress more comfortable than it had ever been. Something was definitely odd. I extracted an arm from my sleeping bag and touched the flooring with the palm of my hand. The synthetic floor was wobbling and sloshy. As I opened my tent door I realised what had happened. The pleasant creek of the previous night, was slowly morphing into a stream and a river. It

- Villa Cerro Castillo, CHILE -

had burst its banks, forming a series of rivulets that branched out from the main course. One of them was now gently flowing past and under my tent, with no Noah's Arc anywhere to be seen. Thanks to some water repellent properties that are well beyond me, the tent had turned into a perfectly sealed dinghy, keeping me all dry inside.

I thought I should skip breakfast and evacuate fast. It wasn't a pretty sight. I tackled the mishap keeping a stiff upper lip despite having to wade through icy waters in a pair of most inadequate plastic slippers. I went back and forth a dozen times, carrying assorted bundles of sacks and belongings to safer ground. Finally I dismantled the tent-raft and breathed a sigh of relief. Wet through to the bone, I started frantically pedalling on a day that was far too miserable to be cycling. The road wound through a lush forest; here and there I spotted stranded cyclists taking refuge in wooden shacks, under tarps or pine trees, but it wasn't a day for stopping and exchanging niceties. I kept moving as if there was no tomorrow, struggling to keep up my body temperature.

Thirty kilometres further, I noticed the unexpected sign of a newly opened Lodge and Resort; it was so new that it hadn't yet made it onto the map I was carrying. It looked rather luxurious to me, but nonetheless I had to find an end to this misery. I walked into the elegant reception area while still dripping. It was only midmorning but Nicholas, the receptionist on duty, welcomed me in. He was a seasonal worker from the town of Conception. He took pity on me, reducing the expensive room rate to a bargain. A pragmatic chap, he knew exactly what was needed; we walked through lengthy corridors and eventually reached the boiler room and a large tumble dryer. A shower and a burger and fries later, my perspective on life had completely changed. It was once again worth living and full of promise. When everything else fails there is always the consolation of not being alone. An hour later it was the turn of two female cyclists from the Netherlands, who walked into reception in anguish. They were dressed in some rubber overalls, looking like they had just emerged from some badly organised scuba diving. Even their wetsuits had failed to cope with the pelting rain. A little later it was the turn of Bob and Rose. They plonked their humid bodies on a couple of chairs right in front of a scolding fire stove. Once partially dried they moved to the restaurant for some late breakfast. From my brief experience it seemed impossible to explore Patagonia without somehow getting very wet. Everyone I had met in the past week was busy trying to dry something.

From then on I refused to believe in more rain forecasts, and it worked. For the first time I basked in warm sunshine, following a particularly spectacular section of the Carretera. Green pastures stretched all around me dotted with spots of wildflowers and burgundy patches of heather. The incredible turquoise waters of Lake General

Carrera loomed in the distance too. I would follow its contours for a few more days on the way to Puerto Rio Tranquilo. The wind, another Patagonian constant, had been kind to me so far; I had only experienced a gentle tailwind that had pushed me along, at times carrying the scents of herbs and spices that perfumed the air. Framing the road on either side were giant leaves of Chilean rhubarb, each one the size of a large opened umbrella. With the village approaching I could also look forward to changing my dreary diet and indulging in some grilled steaks, the pride and glory of South America.

First I had to check in at an 'eco camping' which was quite an experience in itself. Andreas, the guy who was running it, met me as I was walking through the colourful entrance gate. He talked passionately as if he hadn't met any other human being in weeks. He began with a detailed induction into the intricacies of sustainable living and walked me through a series of ten separate recycling bins, each with its own instructions and no exceptions. At the end he pointed with some disapproval to the eleventh one; it had a sign written above it that said 'the shame bin' and only contained an old rusty bedside lamp of course without the light bulb. With all the flying I do for a living, and after today's indulgent steaks, it felt good to be showing a little more respect for the planet.

I woke up to a chilly morning and a tub of Nutella that had turned into a solid block, impossible to spread on a slice of bread. What counted most though was a blue sky that promised well for another day. I had long forgotten the days of feeling like a celebrity while touring in Pakistan. Here it was full of cyclists. I would have gone unnoticed were it not for the fact that nobody was riding a smaller bike than me. Some had come down all the way from Alaska, with wiry and untamed beards. Others had been cycling up and down South America, long enough to become fluent in Spanish. As an Italian and a native speaker of a Latin language, I should have had an advantage, but for some reason my best efforts at Spanish often failed. Sentences turned into an incomprehensible jumble of all the languages

I had ever learned. Every now and then even Japanese words found their way in, together with a little bowing, habits picked up after years of Japanese service.

The dreadful road conditions were made more bearable by the stunning views. Rainfall frequently flooded the soil of the Carretera, creating long stretches of washboard-type gravel. At times it felt as if I was cycling while holding onto a jack hammer. My forearms were furiously shaking while my bum was getting far too intimate with the saddle. I know, one is never quite happy… Only days before, I had cursed all that bad weather and cold, hoping for some sun. Now I was riding in dry and sweltering temperatures, complaining about the heat and wishing it would rain, at least a little. Traffic was sparse and never bothered me, despite the narrow road. I learnt how to synchronise my breathing with each approaching car. As they passed me, I held my breath, disappearing for a few seconds in clouds of smoke and dust.

I spent the night at a campsite run by an old couple, Saturnino and Filomena. All they encountered on their isolated farm hidden behind the top of a hill were cyclists. There were five of us staying. Bob and Rose, regulars I bumped into all the time, and Miguel and Mar, a Spanish couple who were of course appointed as official translators. Both enjoying an early retirement, they were spending two months wandering on their bikes between Chile and Argentina. Miguel used to work in a managerial position at Shell and was a man of the world, having lived in several countries. After a life of expat's benefits and comfort, there was one thing he was now most proud of. He told us with immense pleasure how he had slept under a bridge for the first time, due to a violent storm that surprised them near the town of Futalefu. We sat together in the large dining room eating our meals. Later, Saturnino unboxed a tiny red accordion and played us a selection of *milongas*. It was still early, but each of us disappeared inside our respective tents for a well deserved rest. At 6 am, Rose started her day in earnest. We later heard how she had walked four kilometres each way, to go fishing at a nearby lake. She came back late for breakfast and empty handed. She vented her frustration at having lost the fight with a rainbow trout that managed to wriggle off the hook as she was reeling it in. There was another tough day ahead. I cycled with short stops for about eight hours, climbing and descending mountains. Views always amazed me and kept me entertained. The most spectacular of them all was 'La Confluencia', where the Rio Baker and the Rio Nef crashed into each other in a powerful display of the mighty forces of nature. I reached Cochrane after a series of steep hills in a merciless headwind, exhausted and walking. Half of the journey was now completed, Bronte was still intact. I thought for the first time that I might really make it all the way to O'Higgins, to the end of this derelict road.

- Rio Baker, CHILE -

I liked Chilean people, they were welcoming and kind; if I had a criticism, it was that they didn't seem to care much about tourists. This resulted in a lack of facilities and overall, lousy food. I wondered how different this road would be if it was paved and opened to traffic and tourism. On a bicycle, there was a village every three to four days, with not much in between. Whenever I found something remotely edible, I made sure I ate it. After my start in Coyhaique, Cochrane was the only other sizable village. I shopped at a little supermarket with three aisles of stacked shelves, which felt like a treat. I stocked up with enough supplies to get me through a few more days of want. To be best prepared I gobbled down four empanadas for breakfast before even leaving. These typical snacks of folded pastry contained an assortment of ingredients. Usually hidden inside their fillings were black olives complete with stones that must have kept dentists busy. While locals were surely aware of this, for the general starving traveler, it was like playing a round of Russian roulette with one's teeth.

I left the village loaded with two bags of oats and a half kilo pouch of thick condensed milk. This caloric bomb had been my saviour during the first part of the journey. Outside the town I met a group of five British cyclists from the northern city of Newcastle. One of them was particularly slow and grumpy; his friend later confided that he had been suffering from bouts of diarrhoea. He wasn't quite sure whether it was a result of food poisoning or because of all the dried prunes he had eaten the previous day. Along a spectacular stretch bordered each side by towering mountains, I stopped at a shepherd's hut for the night. Arturo and Luzmira let me pitch my tent in their garden and promised some hot bread and jam for breakfast. In the morning, I watched them curiously as they sat facing each other, in the warmest corner by their wood burning stove. They drank some 'mate', the traditional Argentinian hot drink that is shared from a single hollow gourd. Sipped through a metal straw with holes at the bottom, it looked very much as if they were smoking a pipe. I admired their ability to be at peace without doing or saying anything. As I ate, they sat down for an hour completely at ease in their silence.

That day was my longest so far, covering seventy five kilometres of gravel that took the same effort as double that distance on tarmac. I never got bored; the road took me through forests, along rivers and over mountain passes in which glaciers could almost be touched. Surprisingly I didn't see as much wildlife as I expected, beyond the usual bunch of unwashed cyclists. I met a young couple from France, two Chileans and two young girls from Arizona. The latter were waiting at the bottom of a particularly steep hill, hoping to hitchhike a lift to the top. As far as the British troops were concerned, there were only four of them left. I didn't dare ask about the fate of the prunes man, as he was nowhere to be seen, probably scrambling behind bushes. Beyond Cochrane things got much quieter, with only a dozen cars passing by.

After repeated meals of condensed milk, cold oats, bread, road dust and water, I was on the lookout for something hot and edible. I recognised an isolated farm with a whiff of smoke rising from the chimney. Walking through the gate I approached the door entrance where a few bikes had been parked. Here I met Donna Rosa, busy with frying pans and washing a pile of dishes. She lived in this middle of nowhere, and had made it her mission to serve steaks, hot buns and salad to hungry cyclists. I left the warmth of her simple farm profoundly grateful. Not much further I had a minor mechanical failure that didn't stop me cycling but cost me three of the six gears I had available.

Villa O'Higgins was only a few days away and even if I had had to walk them, nobody could have stopped me. I pushed on in first, second and third gear, and when the grades turned impossible, I just walked. I reached the steepest of climbs as the sun was hitting hardest; a couple of eagles started hovering in circles above me, just in case. I knew I was getting tired because my language became sloppy. I had a grand row with a bunch of aggressive wasps and lost my patience. I realised they weren't listening and burst into a loud 'fuck off!' Luckily no one was around to witness such a pathetic argument.

I made it to Puerto Yungay at seven in the evening, an hour too late to be able to catch the last ferry. As I got closer to the small pier I heard a boat with engines revving. I sped further down noticing the stern ramp still lowered on the cement slip that dived into the water. I waved and shouted to ask if I was in time to get on board. They waved back. Once on board, and just as I was starting to feel lucky, a man asked me whether I had a ticket. Bells started ringing. I knew my short transfer across Mitchell Fjord in order to continue along this crooked journey was a short one and it was meant to be free.

"Where is this going?" I asked.

"Puerto Natales."

This was two days away, on a detour along the Pacific coast. I quickly scrambled back to the metal ramp for a well timed exit without even a thank you. I pitched my tent on the lawn of a tiny wooden church above the pier, waiting for the next morning's departure. The price for a coffee in Puerto Yungay's makeshift bar was on a par with a posh patisserie on the Champs Elysées in Paris. Their best advertising and marketing was the fact that to get another cup of coffee or a pastry one needed to move hundred kilometres either way.

A timely departure at nine in the morning let me cross the fjord and continue along this challenging road. Some irritable wasps decided to join me. At any given time I had about six of them, sitting on my front bag and enjoying the ride. They seemed content while I cycled, enjoying the breeze and all the bouncing, but as soon as I stopped they got all stroppy, starting to buzz noisily around my head. Probably due to the fact that I hadn't had a chance to properly wash in days, they never stung me. I cycled briefly with Francisco, an Argentinian from Córdoba. There were scattered showers and he wore a black waterproof poncho with a pointed hood. At times, strong gusts lifted his caped robe causing it to flutter in the wind. He looked like a Batman on a bicycle, spreading his wings, ready to take off and save the world.

- Casa do Ciclistas, CHILE -

Another long day riding and I reached Casa do Ciclistas just before sunset and in dwindling light. I had read about it before leaving for the trip. It was nothing more than a wooden shack, but it was in a strategic position. It was in the middle of a long stretch of the Carretera without any facilities, and a godsend for cyclists who could find cover, especially on rainy days. It looked unoccupied but I noticed a little smoke puffing up through the chimney. A German man called Gunther had probably heard me rattle on the gravel. He opened the door and welcomed me in. I entered the dark hut, filled with smoke, taking possession of one of the two wide benches on either side.
Gunther was fiddling with a hopeless fire.

"The chimney doesn't work," he said "I am sorry."

A software consultant in his heyday, he was now as dusty as if he had just emerged from a narrow mine shaft. Semi-retired, he lived in the Schleswig Holstein region of northern Germany. He was fond of muddy roads, extreme adventures and polar temperatures. This meant that despite being married, he spent a few months a year cycling on his own. A few years before he had tried introducing his wife to the joys of long distance cycling. He had picked one of his favourite countries, Iceland.

"That didn't go very well, we had bad luck with the weather…" he admitted.

"It was freezing cold, stormy, and we had some issues with food shortages."
"She likes her comforts you know…"

By the end of that trip, one thing was sure: she hated cycling while Gunther learnt to enjoy his own company more and more. As far as holidays were concerned they had found a solution. After he had returned from this rough bike ride they would join a luxurious cruise to the Bahamas.

Gunther particularly loved Patagonia and Iceland; they offered plenty of rain and mud and were his favourite destinations. He was riding this road for the third time. An expert adventurer, he was overloaded with lots of luggage distributed between an oversize bike and a trailer. He was ready to face pretty much anything, as only Germans can. He had run into troubles with stray dogs in the past and carried around his neck a high pitched whistle to scare them. When that didn't work he showed me his next secret weapon, hidden in a small pouch he carried around his waist. I thought it must contain his wallet but instead inside were three round stones ready to be thrown. Unlike me, he had had the odd encounter with wildlife. The day before while camping, he woke up and as he tried to put on his boot he discovered a little snake curled up inside it.

There was a large farm with extensive land behind our decrepit hut. The owner, whom Gunther thought was new as he didn't recognize him, had put the chicken pen right behind it. At five o'clock in the morning, the rooster began to crow loudly. Gunther was vegetarian and gentle natured, but such an abrupt wake-up call played havoc with his nervous system. He stormed out and started to curse in German while beating a stick on a stone. The commotion suddenly stopped. Once he got back inside I asked him whether he had killed the poor bird.

"No." he said, "It's just too much. I hate it."

"At night I went outside and as I entered the little wooden loo, it scared the hell out of me!"

"I was squatting down to relieve myself when I noticed its fluffy feathers shaking in the toilet bowl. I couldn't get it to move and it was all getting too messy so I walked out and went behind the trees instead."

He followed particular dietary requirements that involved carrying all kinds of grains and pulses. He couldn't find steel cut oats, a healthier natural type he was used to eating in Germany. A seasoned Patagonian traveler, one day he discovered that here they are used as animal fodder only. He decided to give these a try, and purchased a large bag from a specialist livestock retailer he had discovered along the way.

"Quality was not that good." he said.

"I even found some stones and dirt inside."
He had dropped the fodder along the road, returning it to the animals it was meant for.

A rest day was called for in Villa O'Higgins. An excellent restaurant with a proper menu and a good selection of delicious dishes reminded me of the simple joys of life. O'Higgins was the last outpost on the Carretera Austral and the final one to be connected in 1999. Eight kilometres further on, by the lake shore, the road ends. This village was officially founded in 1966 but was first settled in the early 1900s by a few English and Chileans pioneers and fugitive convicts. Its remoteness gave it an 'end of the world' aura, maybe not too different from the times of those first homesteaders.

I checked in at El Mosco where about twenty bicycles were parked in a covered hallway. Along its walls were wooden pegs from which hung all kinds of cycling paraphernalia and spare parts, remainders of past adventures and free to be used should one need them. I spent the day resting and chatting to the other guests while watching the rain fall outside. I was lucky not to be cycling. I departed early the following day as a timid sun was rising, covering the landscape with a pale yellow haze. I had to reach the nearby pier in time to catch the ferry that would set off on a three hour journey across Lago O'Higgins. The Carretera was officially over. Cyclists celebrated their personal achievements, photographing their best smiles in front of the road sign. We were now ready to move on to the next adventure. Our bikes were loaded in every available corner, entangled like a jigsaw puzzle. There were probably too many of us, and two bicycles had to be fixed to the bow by means of ropes and expert knots. We reached the other shore and were left to cover the remaining distance to a military outpost, marking the Chilean border, on foot. There were a dozen cyclists and three hikers, getting ready to tackle the most reckless of border crossings. Even before our boat docked, Gunther, with typical German efficiency, was the first to be ready, despite all the stuff he was carrying. He set off on a fast pace, pushing his bike up a steep gravel trail.

I haven't described his bike yet. While it was true to say that I didn't have enough of a bike, he had far too much of one. He rode a carbon fibre monster that looked more like an off road motorcycle with pedals and had a matching price tag. To carry his luggage, he pulled a trailer hooked around its rear frame. We were examples of opposite philosophies. I traveled light to the brink of discomfort, while he carried stuff for all eventualities, ready to cope with each 'one never knows'. A couple of times, while riding behind him, I heard a siren blasting an alarm sound that upset the striking Patagonian silence. Asking what the noise was all about, I discovered that, to match the bike's price tag, he had installed an anti-theft system which ended up being a little temperamental. It was triggered by an over-sensitive remote control button he carried in his pocket. It had not been designed to cope well with the bouncing and shaking and every now and then, set off unnecessary warnings.

We filed into the little military station to have our passports checked and stamped before moving into a sort of limbo, a no man's land where Chile was over while Argentina hadn't yet begun. I followed Gunther up a steep climb that he was tackling for the third time. For a good hour we walked, pushing our bikes up a rocky path. He was fifteen years my senior and had undergone minor heart surgery, yet it was I who struggled to keep up. He steadily disappeared from my sight in the shade of thick groves. If there was an olympic competition for pushing bikes on foot he would have surely won a gold medal. I reached a high plain, then climbed a short hill, the top of which was marked by a metal signpost with the colours of an Argentinean flag.

I had reached the invisible border. Further on, a short ride revealed distant views of the hazy silhouette of Mount Fitzroy. I knew it would be downhill from there but it was far too early to celebrate, the worst part hadn't even started. After brief attempts at cycling I was back on foot. For two more hours, I embarked on a roller coaster of mud, thorny bushes, deep trenches and streams to be forded. It was without a doubt the worst mountain trail I had ever walked, with the added thrill of having to lug around two large bags and a bicycle. The climax was reached when my foot dropped into some quicksand and I began slowly sinking down to my knees. One of my sandals got stuck.

I felt I was breaking its straps as I tried to pull out my leg from such deep mud. I was left with no choice but to slide my foot out and search for it later, as walking the rest of the way semi-barefoot didn't seem a sensible option. So there I was, kneeling down in soft mud and digging with the full length of my arm in order to find it. I admit to some minor swearing that was dampened by the strong Patagonian winds; all lamentations went unanswered. Luckily I did find the footwear and managed to rescue it intact. I emerged from the bushes far from presentable, as if I had survived a mudslide.

On the peaceful shores of Lago del Desierto stood an army barracks with a large flapping flag. The light blue and white stripes confirmed I had made it into Argentina. I looked around for a comment card to fill in but there were none; I would have loved to vent some of my frustration on a bad trail review. A friendly border officer welcomed me instead, probably used to dirty foreigners appearing at his door in tatters and in sour moods. Gunther approached me laughing a little; annoyingly his clothes and shoes seemed unscathed and completely spotless. I waited for the boat and a final lake crossing with a bunch of cyclists. It had certainly not been a grand entrance into this new country, but we were all happy to have survived the ordeal.

The first disappointing impression of Argentina waned as soon as we docked on the other side of the lake. It was soon apparent how different things were here compared to Chile. Argentinians seemed far more accustomed to tourists and they obviously made more of an effort. There were hotels, bars and restaurants just a short bike ride away. I pitched my tent at a quaint campsite just below Huemul Glacier. At night the creaks and groans of the moving ice could be heard, dampened as if they were coming from the belly of the Earth. On my final day it was drizzling and gusty, but all that remained was a downhill gravel road back to civilization. It followed a narrow winding river and the strongest of tailwinds pushed me so hard that it was unnecessary to pedal. Strong gales lifted dust that twisted and twirled, forming spiralling clouds. Bronte was still going strong and, incredibly, in one piece. The unmistakable peaks of Mount Fitzroy got closer and closer, then the distant forms of a village took shape. The constant shaking ended as abruptly as it had started in Cerro Castillo. I climbed up a step and stopped trembling. Everything turned smooth and quiet as I entered El Chalten smiling.

- Mount Fitzroy, ARGENTINA -

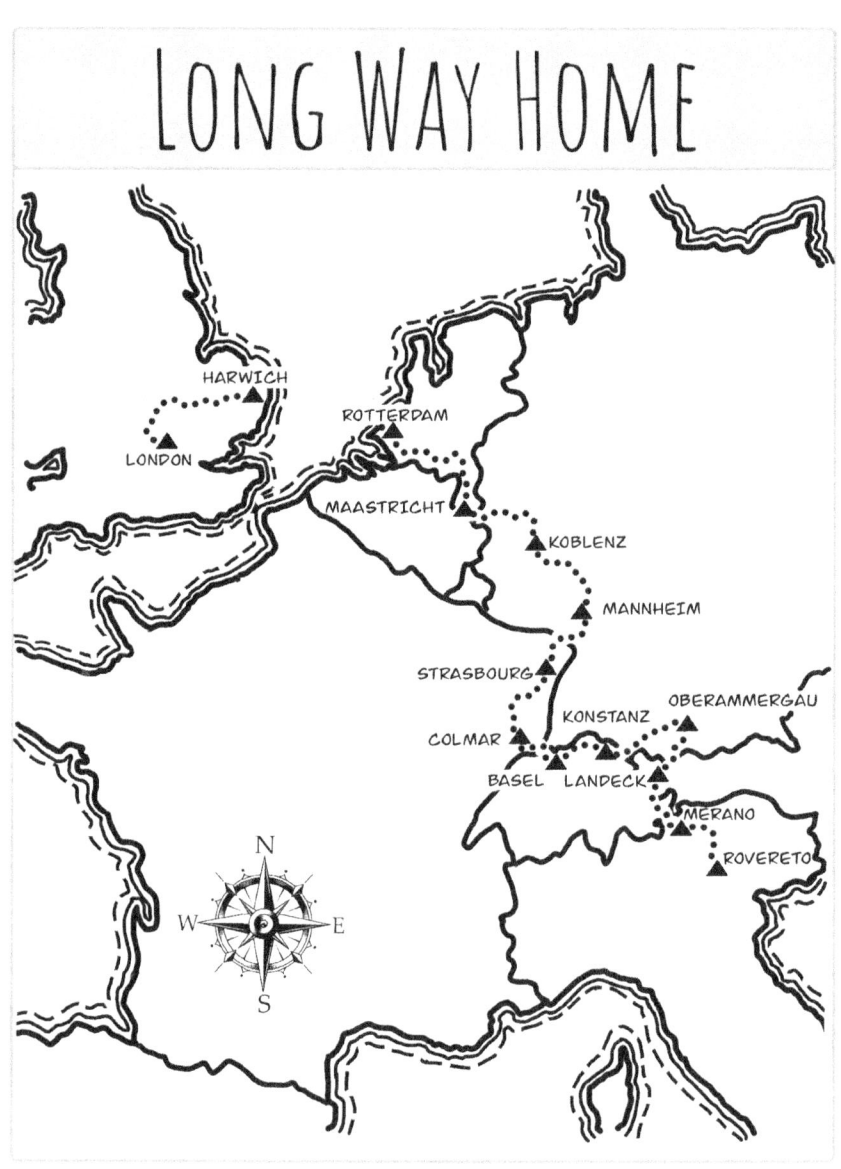

Long Way Home

If there was anything positive about a pandemic that ground the world to a halt with a series of lockdowns, it is that it also allowed plenty of spare time. For many months tourism was transformed into an activity that at most involved pacing up and down a path in the local park or doing countless loops around the neighbourhood. Most looked forward to the weekly visit to the supermarket, finding a common solace in crunchy snacks and pints of booze. By summer I couldn't but feel grateful as the British government turned me, temporarily, into a professional cyclist. Patience had not been in vain; I found myself in the enviable position of being paid monthly for rambling through Europe on a bicycle. In timely fashion, a newer steed had been delivered after months of delays; a brand new black folding bike I called Brutus. It allowed me to retire my old trusted Bronte, who had carried me around plenty of tarmac and some rougher roads too. Without the usual constraints of time, I decided to baptise Brutus by attempting a cycling 'Brexit' to my Italian birthplace. Rules were made on the hoof and constantly changing. Crossing several countries was full of question marks but I thought it would add a bit of suspense and I could do with some fresh air anyway.

By the end of May the countdown was over. I woke up after a stormy night that turned into a gloomy morning; a constant drizzle made me ponder whether I should delay my departure. The ferry ticket to Holland had already been purchased and stopped all dithering, as I had only a couple of days left to reach the port of Harwich. Old bags were strapped around shiny Brutus and we set off from the front door, embracing the wet baptism. Sometimes England throws down rain in buckets but it also has a windy side that leaves hope for a bit of sunshine. It turned out to be the case this time. The courage to face such misery head-on was rewarded a few hours later as clouds gradually parted, revealing some timid sun's rays. Two long months spent mostly inside seemed to have sharpened all my senses. Never had I smelt so clearly the scent of wheat fields as I cycled past them. The first night was a rather windy one, spent in the tent on top of a hill just a stone's throw from Cambridge. Such an ideal spot had been suggested by an elderly lady I had encountered in a village High Street. She hardly looked the part, but in her youth she must have been a wild camper at heart.

"Go back until you pass the chemist, turn right and keep going along the narrow alley." she began.

"You'll reach a metal gate. Go through it and past a red sign and keep walking up the hill following the trail on your right hand side. It takes me half an hour but on your bike it shouldn't take you longer than ten minutes."

"Is it a quiet place?" I asked.

"I think so." she replied.
"I have never seen anyone pitching a tent up there for sure…still, I have always wondered why, as it is glorious up there!" she said, full of enthusiasm, as if she would have liked to join me.

I followed her detailed instructions. I squeezed through a couple of metal gates, passed the large red sign that forbade all camping and followed the trail up a hill covered with a carpet of well trimmed green grass refreshed by the recent storm. I ate something while waiting for dusk to arrive which, close to the summer solstice, took quite some time. For the first hour there was no sign of anyone, but at about eight in the evening the place turned into a hotspot for dog walkers and lovers of sunsets; it was definitely peak time. All kinds of dog breeds walked past me, their owners catching their breath by sitting right next to me on what was the bench with the best view over the valley. I chatted with some, others were more the silent types. One of them was a Welshman, fluent in Italian after having spent four years working in the car industry in Turin. He talked a lot, eager to practise his speaking skills on a native. A couple of passers-by asked if I intended to camp there for the night. I tried to be vague in my answers, but on top of a hill, with the light fading, bundles of luggage all over the place and a bike it was quite obvious that I wasn't waiting for the last train. I waited for the dogs to get tired and for the end of the sunset before hiding in my tent, unnoticed. In the morning I packed everything in haste and walked back downhill towards the village of Orwell, wary that the first perky dogs would soon appear, after successfully dragging out their sleepy owners.

- Cambridge, ENGLAND -

The landscape became as flat as a pancake and the first towers and spires of colleges and churches could be seen in the distance, announcing I was about to reach Cambridge. The town, like everywhere in the country, was in the middle of a lockdown, with all buildings' doors and gates tightly shut; hardly the buzzing place I had visited in the past. Such quietness in towns always elicited a hint of sadness, while the countryside seemed to thrive from that same peacefulness. With reduced traffic and fewer humans disturbing it, wildlife roamed joyfully, having the time of their life. In hindsight, I realised I had left too early in order to meet my ferry's deadline. Maybe it was the fresh memories of my last journey along the troublesome roads of Patagonia where forty kilometres took a whole day and a fair bit of cussing and cursing. Here, roads were flat and nicely surfaced and covering the same distance took a couple of hours. To slow down I enjoyed longer pauses; I mostly spent them sitting on benches in churchyards and cemeteries, calming the restlessness in me that wanted to keep moving. The port was getting closer and so were the Netherlands and my cyclist friend Menno, waiting for me, only a couple of days away.

I made yet another improvised camp in the corner of a large wheat field hidden from the road by a straight line of blackberry bushes. I gambled and stood stark naked, soaking the dust of two days with a sponge bath at sunset. Thankfully, no farmers or dog walkers appeared around the corner. After Cambridgeshire I reached Suffolk and a series of quaint towns and villages whose landscapes had inspired Constable to produce some of his most famous paintings: Sudbury, Bures, Dedham and the river Stour. A long line of cars was stuck in a mighty traffic jam. I asked a driver if anything special was happening. He shrugged and told me they had all come to see the river, as if it was paying them a brief visit on that particular weekend. They were all searching for an elusive parking spot and, if found, formed a zigzagging crowd looking for the perfect spot under an oak tree. Next, down went the blankets, the hampers and the bottles and they enjoyed a few hours of picnicking, ignored by the grazing cows nearby. For the bravest, and it was mostly the children, there was a chance to splash in the fresh waters of the Stour and cool down in the first heat of an early summer.

Climbing a hilly road just outside Stoke by Nayland I noticed a large and elegant Victorian house and on its roof was a tall pole with a Pakistani flag flapping. I thought it was an unusual sight in a remote part of the British countryside. Once in the village, I headed towards the imposing church of St Mary the Virgin that dominates the valley. A lady was tending the garden and I thought I should ask her about it:

"Would you know what the large house down the road with the large Pakistani flag is?"

"A house... with a flag...?" she asked, surprised.
"Where? I have never noticed it..."

"Literally just round the corner. A little further down the road. Huge, green and white with a star and a crescent moon?" I clarified.

She gave me a blank stare and apologised for not being a very good vexillologist, thankfully followed by the explanation that it meant someone who is an expert in flags. Her lack of interest in flapping flags was very well compensated by a sound command of the English language. At Manningtree, the first screechings of seagulls could be heard and the river's estuary pointed me straight to the shores of the North Sea.

An eight hours ferry journey took me to the Hook of Holland and, following England's 'exit' from the Continent, back onto European soil. On the boat, there was a half-hearted attempt by passengers to follow rules and wear masks. It lasted during boarding, but soon everything got sloppy and people confused. Masks were precariously hanging from bent ears or worn under the chins. Kids of course hated them and let it be known with their screams. Once in Holland it was clear that few people still cared about the virus while most fought for their rights, longing for life to return to how it used to be. The long days of June let me cycle into the evening, covering all the forty kilometres to Rotterdam's downtown. Right from the start, it was evident that the country deserved its reputation as a paradise for cyclists; the entire route to my bedroom in the town's hostel was on cycle lanes and far removed from the traffic. I began following the Rhine river that would guide me all the way to the Alpine foothills. Enormous hot houses reminded me of where most fruit and vegetables bought in an English supermarket were ripening. The rest were filled with tulips and all possible varieties of flowers.

After a good rinse, I left Rotterdam in search of Eurovelo 15, or at least the banks of the Rijn as it is referred to in the Dutch language. I thought it would be simple, but near the sea the river gets crazy, splitting into a delta with several branches. I relied on the GPS signal for guidance but that also proved far from accurate. I followed it faithfully, sticking to a green line that twisted on the map of my phone. It left me stranded on a bank I had assumed should be a pier with a ferry crossing the river; There were no signs of either boats or bridges and I was left disappointed, staring at a green line on my phone that continued straight, crossing the river beautifully. Further inland, the river took a more predictable course and I finally spotted the first signposts of a Cycling Route. All other wishes were granted. A blue sky with few clouds, a gentle southerly wind pushing me and, importantly, only a few inches to climb over a hundred kilometres. Each little town or village was picture perfect, its beauty enhanced by the sheer luck of good timing that matched with the full blooms of huge hydrangeas.

Menno lived in Ede, only a short diversion away from the Rhine route and I was really happy to accept his invitation for a place to spend the night. He would then join me for a couple of days on his own, brand new, Brompton bike. Before getting to Ede there were more pretty villages, especially Buren with its nice church tower and windmills; a wonderful bike route towards the town of Rhenen; then the single track dived deep into the forest and I was immersed in a green palette of birches, willows and oak trees. The Dutch did not only seem to take pride in their cycling network, they also rode some amazing bicycles. The cycle route was teeming with life and I frequently suffered the humiliation of being overtaken by grannies with silvery hair, speeding past me without breaking a sweat. I hoped they were riding on electric cycles. In fact, Menno later told me this was becoming more of a problem in the country. The increasing power of electric engines made elderly folks feel young again. They were once again able to reach fast speeds, but their slowing reflexes could easily lead to painful crashes and multiple injuries. Menno worked in a large hospital, so I didn't doubt what he was telling me. Everybody in Holland speaks perfect English, but I had made the error of choosing an orange cover for my rear backpack. Because of that, people launched into long conversations in Dutch while I stared back in silence, waiting for some translation.

 I had cycled with Menno in California, Morocco and, almost, in Utah. Now on his home turf, I happily let myself be guided by him. I turned off my phone and ignored my plans and just stuck close to his back wheel, or at least tried to. He had suggested a diversion away from the Rhine. We veered South and then turned West towards the city of Maastricht, stopping half way at a posh campsite on lake Leukermeer. In Gennep I had to admit that good ice cream was not the prerogative of Italians. We were recommended to try some at a shop on the high street. All they had was a single vanilla cream flavour, but it was to die for. Menno was wearing a futuristic helmet with a combined visor and top-notch aerodynamics that gave him an enormous advantage. At least that is what I told myself, in order to feel a little better; he was ten years older yet I was struggling to keep up with the pace. An authority on everything to do with cycling, at roundabouts or road crossings he had silent conversations with drivers using what seemed to me a mysterious sign language. There were the obvious stretched arms sideways signalling a left and a right turn, but also more advanced gestures. A dangling arm behind him signalled danger, warning me of a possible obstacle. At times he held his hand to the side mimicking a sprinkling of salt; I later learnt that meant debris ahead. The most theatrical gesture was holding his arm high right in front of him, three fingers stretched like a commander spurring his troops to the final assault. I asked him what that meant. Apparently that signalled his intention to go straight at a roundabout. Drivers seemed impressed with such impeccable cycling etiquette; they often saluted him with a short blow of their horn or with their own hand gestures and approving smile. Menno always replied in kind.

The couple of days together had flown by and it was time to say goodbye on the outskirts of Maastricht. We celebrated the occasion by overeating at a Greek restaurant in Geelen. We definitely overdid the grilled meat, the pitta bread, the dip sauces and the french fries. Menno was following a diet that had enabled him to shed considerable weight compared with the last time I met him. By the end of the meal he looked rather worried. The diet involved a mobile app that checked whatever he ate, keeping a daily count of calories; after dessert he started frantically tapping on his phone screen, adding up all the dishes on a sort of food calculator, but then he got stuck on something.

"It's not in the database…" he said, "I just can't find it!"

"How does one spell Souvlaki anyway?"

I told him not to worry too much about it. Whatever the intake, he had cycled all day at olympic speeds I could hardly keep up with. I had no doubt he deserved all the calories.

I saw him off at the local station, from where he planned to return home by train. As for myself, I soon found a farm campsite nearby. A wide open rusty gate led to a field dotted with half a dozen caravans and a couple of tents, but nobody seemed to be around to collect the night fee so I picked a spot and pitched my tent. It got darker and just as I was thinking I might get away with it, an elderly man, who must have been in his nineties, started his walkaround to meet all the guests and collect his due. Remembering faces was obviously not his forte; I met him three times in different places and each time he stopped me and asked whether we had already met and, more important, whether I had already paid.

Despite starting the trip in pouring rain, I had had ten days of glorious weather, more than I would have expected at these latitudes. For this reason I wasn't too upset when I heard from the radio that a thunderstorm was on its way the following afternoon. The morning weather was not too bad and let me roam around the old quarters of Maastricht, buzzing with people shopping and eating. If it wasn't for the hand sanitiser bottles, the masked faces and the signs telling people to follow a very Dutch 1.5 metres distancing rule, all would have seemed pretty normal. I took advantage of the short day I had planned to test the alarm device that Menno had given me to protect my bicycle. Knowing he loved his gadgets I was sure it would be useful. It had arrived by mail from China and consisted of a little black plastic thing, no bigger than a box of matchsticks. The idea was to fix it somewhere on the bike when leaving it unattended and let modern technology work its wonders. The faintest of movements activated an alarm that was not for the faint-hearted. I was amazed at how a few centimetres of plastic could produce such a powerful rattle; it was terrifying. It also came with a remote control with its own little battery. All I needed to do was push a tiny button to put it on standby and it would patiently wait and listen for the slightest movement. I thought it safer to try it out first in the middle of nowhere, before testing it live on the German population. I leant the bike on a fence, put the monster on standby and with a finger just touched the saddle of the bike ever so lightly. Within a split second it blasted out its warning signal as if a nuclear war had just started. Obviously the gadget was really sensitive to movement and it scared the hell out of me and all surrounding wildlife. What had been a quiet rural setting suddenly turned to life; those that could fly took to the sky in an instant and all the rest crawled and scrambled down holes for safety. I was pleased to have tested it and know that the security device had to be treated with the utmost care and respect. True to the forecasts, clouds soon gathered as if from nowhere and in the lovely village of Mechelen I took cover at the local campsite.

What a beautiful thing Europe is. If it wasn't for the fact that registration plates suddenly turned from orange to white and cycleways turned a bit shabby, I wouldn't have known that I had moved into a different country. I had crossed the border into Germany down a narrow country lane that eventually led me to the town of Aachen. After the diversion to get back to the Rhine, I cut across a series of steep hills which were a complete shock after ten days of nothing but plains. I was struggling to find an open campsite, so I kept pushing on. After the hundred kilometres mark, which in my experience is when things start to get a bit uncomfortable, I spotted a suitable lawn between long lines of pear and apple trees.

I rejoined the river a couple of hundred kilometres further south than where I had left it. Cutting a good portion of the continent from north to south, the Rhine has for centuries been the chosen route for boats and long barges carrying all kinds of heavy loads. I was slow on my folding bicycle, but going upstream made me faster than them; my frequent stops to appreciate wonderful cheesecakes meant that we kind of travelled together, keeping each other company. It turned out that Holland had been pretty relaxed about the whole virus thing. Germany was still throwing the kitchen sink at it. Entering a shop without wearing a mask was done at one's own peril. I crossed the city of Koblenz, a mix of ugly industrial sites on the outskirts and beautiful houses, forests and parks along the riverside. The further south I travelled the more the scenery became interesting, with the cycleway winding through a series of forests and castles, perched up on the mountains all around me. I made my second river crossing thus far by ferry, and checked in at a campsite where the host, bored from the lack of tourists, invited me to join him for a barbecue he had planned with some friends.

- Bacharach, GERMANY -

Days turned a little cloudy as I passed through a string of attractive villages: Biebernheim, Oberwesel, Bacharach, historic treasures always enhanced by the most generous displays of flowers. More importantly for a cyclist, each had its own old bakery with freshly baked breads and pastries. The thirsty and the rowdy would not agree with me, but the best reason to visit Germany is not beer but its baking skills. As for protein, it was provided for free by nature, thanks to the bad habit of cycling with my mouth slightly open. In the first heat of summer, I passed through clouds of insects, so tiny that even the fussiest of entomologists would not bother studying. The lucky ones ended their meaningless lives drowned in gastric juices.

I noticed a trend in cyclists riding with loud speakers. They mostly blared out German techno music all the way back from the eighties. As if this wasn't bad enough, the music reached my ears distorted by motion as they passed me. Just as I was about to overtake a long boat called Josef Langen, it started pouring and I took temporary cover under a tunnel. I hoped it would be a short cloudburst, but in the end I gave up waiting and faced it. Something irrational happens each time I willingly push on, cycling under the rain. I feel brave like a hero, as if raindrops could hurt me. Eventually it pelted down seriously, and I stopped feeling heroic and hid once more inside a second tunnel. Miraculously the weather cleared in a matter of minutes. At Bingen, the Rhine Route turned suddenly sloppy and disappeared in a messy mud as I entered the forest. I lost the river too for a little while but found a Chinese man to chat to instead, or to try to. On his bike he was carrying what looked like a regular suitcase, as if he was heading to the airport to catch a plane. There was no chance of communicating beyond gestures and lots of laughter, but he resorted to a translating app he had installed on his phone. He spoke some Mandarin to his phone and after a short delay the English translation started playing from the speakers. Sentences didn't make much sense but he enjoyed using it.

"Let me have peace in the Alps." said the digital voice, reproachfully.

I wondered whether I had upset him.

It took some time to try and figure out what he wanted to tell me. After a few more comically dismal attempts he showed me a map and I figured out what he was trying to say. He was heading to the Swiss town of Lugano, whether in search of peace I would never know. After the rough morning storm I couldn't believe my luck in being able to enjoy a swim in a forest lake by the evening. Refreshed and with the day's sweat cleansed off, I fell asleep listening to the gentle calls of a cuckoo sitting on a nearby tree.

Oppenheim marked the thousand kilometre milestone. The sun was out all morning, so bright that for the first time I thought I would take out my solar panel and charge my batteries. Attached to it, in order to keep the panels from flapping around or closing, was my New York State registration plate that confused the public. Coffee places and restaurants had a new set of rules to follow. Before ordering anything it was necessary to register with a full address and telephone number. To perpetuate the illusion, I got into the habit of writing down my English pseudonym John Phillips. Next, I needed a suitable New York City address; the only one I could vaguely remember was an hostel address I once stayed in: 52 Amsterdam Avenue, Manhattan, 10025 New York. A bit naughty, but this was something intended to enable the authorities to get in touch in case of an infection, and as a rambling cyclist it seemed rather pointless. They would have to chase me down the Rhine route, and on a bicycle with flashing sirens.

Eurovelo 15 turned briefly inland as I caught up with an elderly man in his eighties. He was cycling slowly, taking up the full width of the single lane with an electrically powered tricycle. No amount of bell ringing succeeded in alerting him of my presence behind. Age must have played tricks with his hearing and even a crescendo from the Berliner Philarmoniker Orchestra would have gone unnoticed. I contemplated setting off my Chinese alarm system to warn him, but that would have been unkind. I relaxed instead, accepting a gentler pace, cycling behind him for a good ten minutes before taking advantage of an overtaking opportunity. The long necks of cranes stuck out through the tall grasses in the fields around me; at times I would involuntarily scare them and they would rise in flight, lending their magnificence to the sky. Cycling along the Rhine was not always pretty. As is usually the case, there was also an ugly side to it. Providing easy access to large ports and the sea, it acted as a magnet to factory complexes that were built right on its banks. Hours were spent cycling through the unremarkable outskirts of cities like Mainz, Worms and Mannheim, going past steel plants, concrete chimneys and grey walls covered in a mess of graffiti. I sped through such places, eager to get back to the fields and the little villages that were close but seemed a world away. I indulged in milk, fresh bread and thick layers of Nutella chocolate spread, one of my favourite childhood breakfasts. Nutella also works well as a temperature forecast; when it spreads easily on bread early in the morning, it is always the sign of an ideal temperature.

I admired the flight of two cranes; they were playing with thermals and currents on a synchronised flight that resembled a dance. There were more invisible borders as I moved into France. I wondered how the French were coping with the spreading virus. Here *liberté, egalité et fraternité* still held true despite everything that was happening. The wearing of face masks was advisory only. The major change was that I could brush up my knowledge of the French language and was finally able to understand what was said around me. Half way through a month on a bicycle, it was time to have a rest day and prepare for the next leg. Lauterbourg, the first village I encountered across the border, turned out to be an ideal place; I checked into its excellent municipal campsite just by a large artificial lake. Crowds were swimming and enjoying themselves as though on a normal summer's day.

In this border town where wars had been fought in the past, one could now easily cross between France and Germany just to do some shopping. That is exactly what I did in the morning, just for the thrill of it. I had planned to buy plenty of food and some proper swimming trunks to get ready for a day of swimming in the Bassin de Mouettes. Once back in France, I realised I had carelessly bought a pair of trunks sized for a twelve year old, which I could raise as far as my knees. In what turned out to be a busy morning, I went back into Germany to find out whether they could be exchanged, but once there, it dawned on me that I had forgotten my muffler, which I would normally use to cover my nose and mouth and avoid being shouted at. A day in France had been enough to make me forget all about it. I didn't want to go back and forth between nations more than necessary so I started rummaging through my bag. All I had was a clean pair of grey underpants. I folded them in half, squeezed the openings through the neck, and wrapped them tight around my nose and mouth. There are times when you appreciate being a complete stranger in a foreign town! What I was most worried about was bursting out laughing at the checkout. I joined the queue and waited patiently for my turn; once facing the cashier in order to pay I could tell that she knew something odd was on my face. To make matters worse, German bureaucracy threw a spanner in the works. To get a refund some paperwork was involved. A longish queue built up behind me while I completed the form as fast as I could, worried that my loose pants would drop down. It all worked out in the end. I made a hasty exit, maybe leaving everyone wondering whether that weirdo had just been shopping with a pair of underpants wrapped around his face.

Eurovelo 15 continued and was now called Route du Rhin with a welcome French flair. The river marked the border with Germany and crossing a bridge was a big deal, as in a matter of minutes I could go from a place where I could communicate as an adult to one where I had the eloquence of a newborn child. After a couple of weeks of endless horizons I was surprised to notice the first profiles of the Vosges mountains appear in the far distance. Life was being kind to me. All I could whinge about were trivial matters; not finding a bench and a table when hungry, or having to endure the incredible smells of french meals floating in the air at lunchtime. France responded to German cheesecakes with its renowned cheese shops and bakeries. The latter were everywhere and their warm croissants and arrays of pastries were a blessing to every worn out cyclist. After crossing a long forest trail, I emerged in the suburbs of Strasbourg. It was thirty years since I had spent a wonderful summer there. I wandered around the city centre, trying to rekindle long lost memories, but all I could remember were the imposing gothic cathedral and the old quarter of La Petite France with its cobblestone streets, canals and half-timbered houses. I stopped by the information office, where they suggested I should quit the river and continue along the renowned Route du Vin instead. It is a twisty road through wineries and a handful of charming villages and, as I recalled, one of the highlights of the region. All I remembered from thirty years ago was doing it on board a tourist bus, which had left me blind to almost everything.

I left Strasbourg late, cycling along the Canal de la Bruche, and close to eight in the evening started looking out for a good spot to rest. A side road led me to a field and a large patch of grass shielded from views by bushes and trees. I had slept between vineyards, wheat fields, rows of apple and pear trees, and it was time to sleep in a corn field. It is referred to as 'stealth camping', a name I am not too fond of as it sounds a bit criminal. It means a complimentary stay under the stars, when one is lucky, and it comes with its own set of rules that must be followed: set camp at dusk or just before night time, leave at dawn, choose a place that is hidden, away from walkways, towns and villages. Of course never leave any trace or rubbish. Ideally one should not be seen because that increases the risk of getting into trouble. I laid down my bags and bike, sat on the grass and started to eat. For a good hour nobody was heard or seen. It seemed a promising place. At twilight I had all the confidence I wouldn't be disturbed so I began pitching my tent and settling down.

As I was ready to relax the place started buzzing with families, small children, lovers in search of a hideout, night runners and the ever present dog walkers. It was too late to move anywhere else and I ended up having a chat with quite a few. A young couple, who had obviously not noticed me, settled down with their blanket behind the bushes; out of courtesy I said a *bonsoir*. This was obviously a bit of a spoiler; it scared the hell out of the bloke, leaving the lady slightly disappointed and surprised to realise that after all, she was not dating such a brave man. They moved away, in search of better bushes where they would not get disturbed. What families with toddlers were doing walking in corn fields at night-time escaped me. I could sense parents warning their kids not to approach me, as I must have looked like danger. I pretended not to see them. A little girl wouldn't have any of it.

Fascinated by my tent she sprinted towards me while her mom followed her shouting in a panic. She grabbed her hand and scolded her as if she had just risked being murdered. Once it got really dark it was the turn of two night joggers. Surprised to see my tent appear in the dim light of their head torches they took a detour and started running faster. Finally, a young chap passed by walking his puppy. It is pointless trying to hide from dog walkers; they tend to appear from nowhere in the most unexpected of places at ungodly hours of the night or morning. He started chatting to me. Out of politeness, I asked whether he thought I was bothering anybody by pitching my tent.

"How long?" he asked me, as if I was planning to move into the cornfield indefinitely.

"Just the one night." I replied to his obvious relief.

"I am not sure about the law," he told me, "but you should be fine…" and that was fine with me.

The ride acquired its own soundtrack. Maybe out of feeling a little lonely, as I sped through vineyards I started remembering the notes of 'Douce France', an old classic by Charles Trenet that I was taught in my first year learning French at school. A pleasant song really, rather harmless until one gets addicted and hums it in a loop all day. I couldn't get it out of my head and, only remembering the chorus, it began to sound rather annoying.

'…*Douce France, cher pays de mon enfance, bercée de tendre insouciance, je t'ai gardé dans mon coeur… Mon village au clocher aux maisons sages…*'

The Wine Route was more hilly than the river but rich in interesting villages. Molsheim was one of these; I discovered, to my surprise, that between bakeries and cellars, an Italian migrant named Bugatti had started building his famous cars that could reach speeds of over two hundred kilometres per hour in the 1930s. Part of the route at times joined the Via Francigena, an ancient Roman road. Each town clung to the top of a steep hill, following gradients that taught me something about the Romans; they certainly did not ride bicycles. After half a day of strong headwinds I was exhausted, forgot all about history and the twisty Francigena and picked the straightest, more boring road I could find on my map.

´*...Douce France, cher pays de mon enfance...*' darn it!

I was still singing it; it was way too cheerful a song for a day spent cycling over hills and against gusty headwinds. The postman on his motorbike heard me singing it as he was overtaking and started laughing. Unlike most tourists, I left the Wine Route without having had a taste of it. All I did was smell the sour scent of juices ripening in wineries. Dietrich, a seventy years young German cyclist I met at the campsite in Turckheim, came to my rescue and offered me a glass from the daily bottle he was having. He was on a journey of three thousand kilometres around Europe, and in a matter of twenty minutes as we were chatting, he ate a baguette with goat's cheese and finished the rest of a bottle of Riesling. His age and fitness level made me realise that wine can't be that bad after all, and I wondered whether I should start drinking. He was from Munich and, as I was about to head that way, I thought I should ask him how best to navigate around Bodensee. All that Riesling made him very talkative; he pulled out a series of maps from his luggage and for one hour, went into minute detail on what his favourite five ways would be. The fact that he spoke only German, with a few words of English thrown in, meant that all those straights, lefts and rights got a little jumbled in my mind, but I was grateful he had given me some ideas.

Maybe Holland's flatness had turned me into a weakling but I couldn't help noticing how reaching each village meant climbing a very steep hill. The cycle route signposts lead me to the top of each one of them, to then misguide me, and leave me cycling around in circles. The cynical in me thought it must be some sort of marketing ploy, ensuring tourists would eventually buy something. After visiting the picture perfect town of Colmar I crossed the Rhine and returned to Germany. On this side the route followed the river closely in what turned out to be one of the best parts of the entire journey. The trail I followed was mostly unsurfaced but as smooth as a pool table. At the end of the day, I noticed that the only campsite seemed to be on the French side. I crossed back and at a certain point realised that I was standing on the borders of three countries all at once. The borders of France, Germany and Switzerland converged under my wheels, respective flags confirming it. As for the French campsite, it was a fiasco as the gate was firmly shut displaying a closed sign. By way of another bridge I returned to Germany en route to Lorrach. Eventually the road was blocked by custom police checking traffic but I whizzed around the queue of cars and crossed the Swiss border. After finding a campsite the first question I asked the lady at the check-in booth was which country we were in. Generally, this is a question that could get one fast-tracked into a psychiatric ward, but around here it was not uncommon. She laughed before telling me that, of course, we were in Germany.

Past Basel, the river veered east, flowing between Germany and Switzerland. By now I was really enjoying the freedom of choosing on a whim which country to ride in. To avoid the high prices, it meant eating and sleeping in Germany while cycling most of the day in Switzerland. At a roundabout a driver slowed down alongside and shouted 'God Bless America', which left me a little puzzled. I had completely forgotten about the New York registration plate on display at the front of the bike, a sort of talisman. I had carried it along on my Ladakh trip, as well as in Patagonia, and by now I had complete faith that it was thanks to that length of tin that I hardly experienced any mechanical failures. For obvious reasons I hadn't carried it in Pakistan and I almost ended up killing myself. I still think that was not too bad a decision, as I am not sure displaying a US plate in that country would have been the best travel insurance.

After those experiences, and despite not being that superstitious, I have always taken the view that I should bring it along, just in case. There was more excitement on the way. I crossed a short iron bridge that brought me to a thin island that stretched for miles, running parallel in the middle of the river. For the first time, my right leg was pedalling in Switzerland while my left one was steadily on German soil, and it wasn't painful.

Later that same day, the route left the banks of the Rhine, Rhein or Rijn and started rolling over gentle hills, not far from Zurich airport's flightpath. I stopped, watching a few planes as they were about to land, hoping for normal life to return. Down south, the snowy peaks of the Alps were floating above the haze, and beyond them was my country. I stayed on the left bank of the river, but at a certain point Switzerland must have invaded a corner of Germany. Scattered on a hilly plateau were some of the most charming villages, vast rolling meadows interrupted by yellow patches of sunflowers. Germany fought back, and without me crossing any bridges I was once again in the BundesRepublik, or at least I thought so. I entered a charming village and on the sidewalk noticed a pair of legs with a bent torso disappearing into a thicket of bushes. An elderly man seemed to be carrying out some kind of extreme gardening. I waited for him to emerge from the mess he had got into and thought I would ask one more time which country we were in. He dusted himself down a little before giving me a convoluted answer. It was in German, but I think I got the gist of it. Apparently we were geographically in Switzerland but politically still in Germany. Further explanations followed and things got too complicated; he then started waving his hands erratically and shrugging his shoulders which gave the impression that it was just a total mess and, after all, even he himself was not too sure.

A group of Italian cyclists overtook me; they were on fast racing bikes, also wary of the Swiss Franc and eager to find a way out of the country. In Schaffhausen, the Rhein tumbles down some of the most powerful waterfalls of the continent.

- Schaffhausen, SWITZERLAND -

Dietrich, the elderly German who was cycling on Riesling, had told me that despite not being quite the Niagara Falls, they were still impressive. A large crowd of tourists paced the walkways around them searching for the best views. Further east the Rhein got wider before merging into the Bodensee or Lake Constance, a lake that would accompany my ride for a couple of days.

I passed Konstanz, riding a scenic route wedged between the lakeside and the railway and headed towards Bregenz as the German Alps rose higher in front of me. Late afternoons on sunny days often ended with dips in the lake before starting a leisurely search for a decent spot for wild camping. This trip had really tested me, revealing over and over again my lack of geographical knowledge. Once again, I found myself in the wrong country. What I was convinced should be a straightforward border crossing into Germany, turned out to be the Austrian border instead. It was just a little teasing of Austria, marking the sixth country reached so far. It took barely an hour of cycling to move back out of Austria as I reached a signpost that welcomed me to Bayern. I said my final farewells to the Rhein in Bregenz, where it took a sudden turn to the west and away from my plans. I reached the tail end of Lake Constance as a storm was about to head my way. The alpine landscape marked an abrupt change. It was mostly pine forests, rolling hills and herds of large grazing cows. Now that I did not need to stick to a river, I could pick and choose the cycleways I most fancied.

I found the perfect place to weather a storm in a campsite with good facilities and its own private lake. To start with it did not seem promising. On my arrival I was told it was only opening the following day and that it was fully booked anyway. I took on the role of the shattered cyclist that worked magnificently, bending rules even in such a strict country. The owner accepted cash only, asking me to keep it quiet and confirming, once again, my conviction that bicycles work wonders. I shared the peaceful alpine lake with a handful of other guests that I assumed were relatives, staff or, rather like myself, illegal customers. The windy night followed by rainfall dropped the temperature but only a few streaks of clouds remained by the morning. I was ready to roll over the hills of Bavaria. It got stormy again in Elbsee, but this had been accurately forecast, allowing me to plan a day's rest at another campsite. I checked in early in the afternoon, loaded with plenty of snacks and groceries. After an afternoon swim, clouds started gathering and I took cover in my tent as the first rumbles of thunder began. It poured down heavily throughout the night and into the early morning, so I spent the time resting my legs and munching unusual quantities of crisps and chocolate biscuits.

I woke up to a chilly morning and dense fog, with the tent's flysheet soaking wet. I was struck by the kindness of Bavarian farmers, who didn't seem to bother much about erecting fences to delimit their properties. Gone were the gates, the barbed wire and all the hedges; and gone were the usual signposts threatening dire consequences if trespassing. What was left was a more inviting, open and green farmland. I followed parts of the Romantische Straße and headed south, towards towering mountains that stared right into my face. The initial climb seemed kind and gentle and led me, without too much effort, just short of the thousand metre mark and the town of Oberammergau. A road sign reminded me of all the good reasons why, decades earlier, I had given up learning the German language. On it was an unpronounceable word, 24 letters long:

'Abfallentsorgungszentrum'.

I later learnt it meant 'Waste disposal centre', and I must say I would rather have it the English way, broken into separate parts, allowing one to catch one's breath a little.

    I left Oberammergau and was looking forward to my next destination, the famous winter resort of Garmisch Partenkirchen. As the road took a sudden turn, I caught my first glimpses of the impressive rock face of Zugspitze, the highest mountain in the country. Most of the day was spent cycling around it, before moving into Austria, this time for a little longer. Two further mountain passes needed crossing before reaching Italy. The first and the easiest one was Fernpass; it took Brutus above the thousand metre mark for the first time. At the top of the pass I sat on a bench and was joined by a German entrepreneur who was also an avid cyclist. He was the founder of a bike courier company that he said was growing in popularity across his country. He was fascinated by my unusual bike and, looking at all the luggage, asked whether I was also delivering something.

    The descent from Fernpass was steep and with lots of traffic and so demanded all my focus and attention. Lower down the valley, I moved to the relative safety of a cycle route that twisted through shady pine forests. Before Imst I glanced at my odometer and realised I had just passed the two thousand kilometre barrier. I stopped in Landeck, at the foot of Reschen pass, and this was a good starting point from which to climb up to the Italian border the following day.

I was keen to cross the Alps, but it turned out to be less straightforward than I had imagined. I followed the Via Claudia, climbing to about the halfway point. A German cyclist had warned me that the main road was not recommended because of long tunnels and traffic. Sure enough I soon met the first road signs warning cyclists to take their bikes elsewhere. The only alternative was to head towards the village of Martina. The name sounded very Italian, but the steep descent sent me right back into Switzerland. Not knowing which country you are going to end up cycling in on a given day is hardly a testament to good preparation and planning. Another slight annoyance was that I had gone mostly downhill and I knew that meant I would have to start climbing all over again. At least the one lane road was peaceful and interesting, with so many bends that it turned out to be twice as long; eventually, it took me back into Austria, where it merged with the main road I had left earlier. I was on top of the pass by lunchtime. The familiar *tricolore* flag and a border sign confirmed that I had made it all the way to my own country. Not that one would notice. The Alto Adige province was for centuries part of Austria and one has to go a little further into Italy to hear the Italian language. As a child I remember once seeing on the cover of a travel magazine the picture of a church tower emerging from the turquoise waters of a lake. Almost by chance a few decades later I was right in front of it. The artificial lake of Resia, constructed in 1950 to produce electricity, had in the process submerged a few villages. All that remains visible now is the medieval church tower of Curon, rising out of the waters as if catching its breath.

I had spent weeks allowing rivers to guide me. The Rhein, but also the Maas, in Holland, the Isar and Loisach in Germany and the Inn in Austria. Mount Resia is the source of Adige, the second largest river in

Italy, and it flows through my birthplace. Sticking to either bank of this final river would lead me straight to my hometown of Rovereto. It was still some distance, a mileage that should have taken a further two days, but being close gave me a rush of adrenaline. I followed the river downhill at great speed, curious to see how far Brutus could take me. The mountains' profiles took the familiar shapes of a road I must have cycled hundreds of times. A cyclist's friend joined me for the final stretch, as the strong southerly wind, habitual in the afternoon, welcomed me. It started drizzling and I felt tired, but I had made it all the way back home and I couldn't have been happier.

- Passo Resia, ITALY -

Southern England

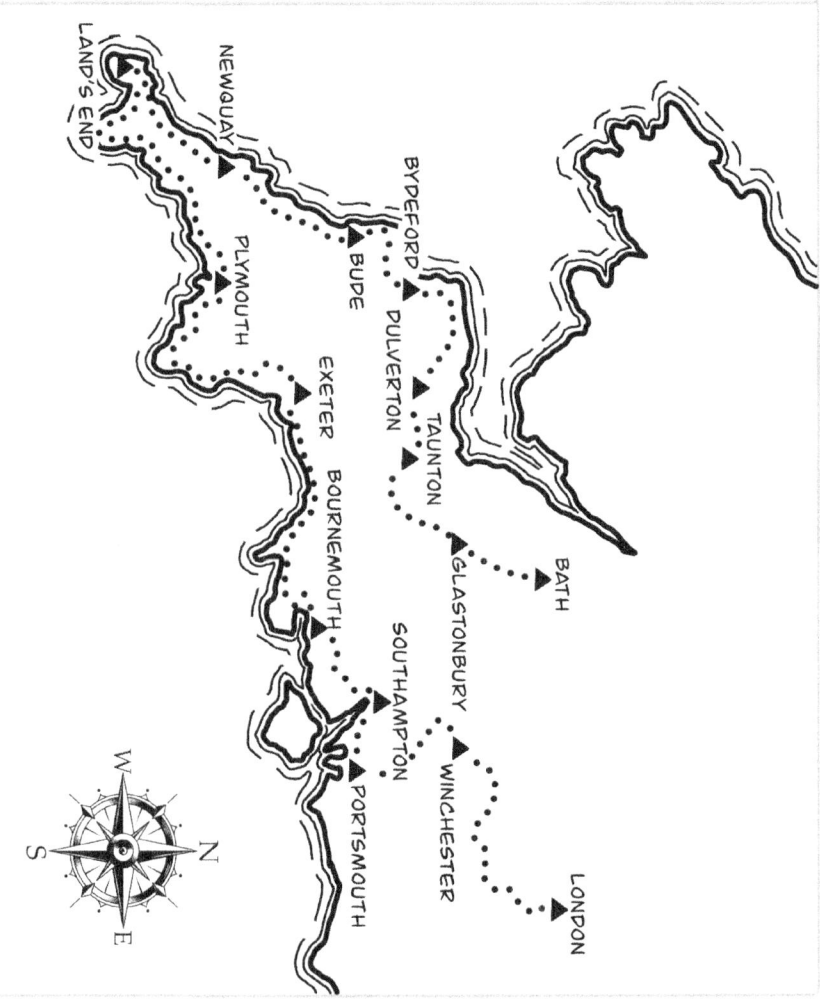

Southern England

A year on and the virus is still happily reproducing, and doing so at increasing speed. They have thrown everything but the kitchen sink at it, confined people in 'bubbles', with faces behind masks, yet the plague remains strong, infecting people extremely effectively. There seems to be some light at the end of the tunnel: vaccines in all flavours have finally arrived! For some it's been a tragedy, for most a misery, but something good has also come out of it: the chance to rediscover and reconnect with nature. We have all become part-time twitchers or passionate photographers. After months indoors, folk who would hardly have noticed anything beyond their phone screen, are happily lying on all fours to snap that perfect reflection of morning dew in a blade of grass. Ducks and squirrels couldn't have had it better. For them it's been a year of bounty; the relentless feeding by park visitors, who before had a job to go to, has left them on the verge of obesity. Dogs have gone from missing their owners all day to becoming overwhelmed by all the love and attention, and exhausted by multiple daily walks.

I had always meant to tour England but so far had put it off due to a profound distrust of the weather. Now I had plenty of time and the great advantage of starting the ride with a good forecast. The trusted BBC weatherman announced an unheard of two weeks dry spell. I took it with a pinch of salt, but even if it turned out to be sunny for just a couple of days, it seemed a pity to waste it. It was April, still chilly, so I thought I should start in the South. The morning of my departure was glorious and sunny. Andrea joined me for the first day out of London, all the way to a tent spot on a heath near Dorking. Not as exciting as our climbs over Ladakh's mountains, but I was happy to have his expertise in navigating London's suburbs while avoiding traffic. I met him at Blackfriars Station and, as he was taking a few photos with his camera, I heard my name being called: a chance encounter with Susan, another passionate Brompton tourer. We had only communicated online via comments left on videos of our respective journeys, but she had recognised me, maybe helped by the brim hat with a Union Jack flag stitched on it.

Near Dorking, Andrea turned back for his return trip. Just as the sun was setting, I found a place to pitch my tent at Farley Heath, in the company of a couple of pheasants and a small buck, who glanced at me, curious, and then mostly ignored me. At midnight I woke up shivering from the cold, compounded by a chilly wind. By 1 am I had run out of socks to wear and by 3 I was just about coping, wearing a coat and a couple of jumpers and cursing myself for not bringing the new, warmer sleeping bag I had left back home. The BBC's promises were fulfilled on the second day as I continued along the Surrey Hills, in a valley between the North and the South Downs. I had cycled most of these roads long ago on regular weekend outings. There were lots of *deja vus*, with roads and landmarks that looked vaguely familiar, but having cycled many roads since then, I could have easily been deceived and it might as well have been a similar road in a different continent.

A tour is never complete without a camping fiasco and I thought I would start early. Finding an open patch of grass in this part of the country proved harder than I had imagined. All I could see were fences upon fences, and then the town of Winchester came into view. After paying a visit to the wonderful cathedral, daylight was fading and the situation was getting quite desperate. When I felt it was too dark to continue, I climbed over a fence and scrambled up a hill through tall grass, trespassing on land belonging to an energy company. I had a good view over the lights of Winchester but was far too close to a busy section of the motorway. To improve my bad mood, I had just bought a large portion of fish and chips, which by the time the tent was ready had turned cold and soggy.

- Winchester, HAMPSHIRE -

I woke up early the next morning, recalling that I was on private property and I ought to pack and leave early. Unzipping the tent's door I realised there was nothing to worry about. A thick and freezing fog was covering the town below me and I could take all the time I wanted. The cold lasted for most of the morning as I set off cycling, wearing everything I carried. I wish that by living in England, I had acquired a bit of the Brits' endurance and stamina that allows them to wear clothes according to the season rather than to match the day's temperatures. For the natives, mid April is good enough to go sleeveless and in short trousers, and to forget all about socks; remarkable in a country where it can snow in the summer or be rather mild in January. In the freezing fog of the early morning I saw several cyclists and runners, upholding this peculiar tradition. While I was shivering in my plump winter gear, I passed them full of admiration.

Their faces, forearms and legs, exposed to the elements, ranged from purple to the colour of a boiled lobster; they pushed on with bravery, on the verge of hypothermia, clad in razor thin lycra.

After Southampton, I criss-crossed the trails of that peaceful haven, the New Forest, before reaching a cosy room in a bed and breakfast in England's retirement Mecca that is Bournemouth, at a place run by Christina and her family. The only other guest was David, a retired man from Bournemouth. When I arrived they were all chatting in the garden and I assumed they were relatives; I was told he would show me around as well as see me out the following morning. The real story was more complicated. He had sold his house a month earlier, planning to move into a new one, when the pandemic struck and other things went awry and he found himself wealthy and homeless. With a healthy pot of savings, he checked in at Christina's place for a week in order to search for an alternative house. A month and a half had passed and he was still searching. He told me he was a keen birdwatcher and also loved walking. He knew the area perfectly and, looking at my map, agreed with most of what I had planned; and promised I would be pleased with the days ahead of me.

I left not too early the following morning, cycling along the beach stretch to Sandbanks, where a chain ferry took me across to the Isle of Purbeck. Gigantic cruise ships were anchored at sea, waiting for better times not too far from the coastline while saving the expense of a long mooring in Southampton. On a sunny day, National Cycle Route 2 was one of the nicest cycleways I had ever cycled. It crossed an extensive peninsula owned by the National Trust, which had turned it into a nature reserve inhabited almost exclusively by grazing cattle and cute ponies. I followed its trails for a couple of hours during which the only humans met were three cyclists and a couple of ramblers. That peace and quiet then vanished. A series of bomb blasts shook the earth, scaring birds and cyclists, and I figured out I was alongside a mock up war-zone used by the military. David had warned me, saying that I might hear loud explosions and gunfire, but that I shouldn't worry too much about it. Having left some of the most exquisite countryside, I was suddenly in a wasteland where army recruits expressed their angst by throwing hand grenades and bomb, and shooting fake bullets at each other. David had also told me that a little further on was Burton Bradstock, where I would certainly find a nice patch for my tent, on top of white cliffs overlooking the Channel. The pitch was right by the cliff edge a few steps away from a fifty metres vertical drop to the sea. I put bike and belongings to my right side, blocking the exit as a reminder: 'if you need to pee at night, please exit from the safe side'. It was a world apart from the Winchester emergency camp, with plenty of time to savour an epic sunset and spend a night lulled by the rolling waves.

The pandemic still raging, travelling meant coping with unexpected challenges. I was about to run out of water over the hills of Dorset and, noticing a young man by the gate of his farmhouse asked whether I could fill up my large bottle.

"Sure!" he said in a friendly manner, "just come in."

His dad joined in on the excitement of a cyclist with a weird accent. They walked me through their garden and I handed dad my bottle, waiting by the entrance. He briskly walked inside and about a minute later a kerfuffle started up. His wife was not happy and stormed out of the kitchen shouting:

"No! No! You can't!"

"The virus!" she reminded him, as if no one was aware of it.

He came back to the door looking a little sheepish and returned my bottle, still empty. His wife calmed down and apologised to me while thoroughly sanitising the hands of her husband and instructing him on the correct way of proceeding. He returned a few minutes later with

one of his own plastic bottles and transferred water from vessel to vessel, each of us holding his own bottle. I apologised for breaking the family peace and he shrugged, with a twinkle in his eyes.
While not denying the suffering, I can't help feeling that the pandemic has been blown out of proportion. At times I have met individuals who have gone to the extreme of turning their head to the opposite side as they pass, as if PEST is written in capital letters on one's forehead.

I ate my fourth meal of fish and chips. Fried food is not ideal for a cyclist but along these coastal towns that is all they seem to eat for lunch and dinner, and they would inevitably recommend it. It happened again this lunchtime. Reading the menu at a delicatessen shop I was determined to get their steak and kidney pie, but the lady at the counter wouldn't have any of it and discouraged me.

"I would have cod if I were you..." she said.
"We have a special batter recipe that is crispy and sublime." she continued.

Once again, I fell for it. With lunch over, an excruciating climb awaited me just outside the town of Sidmouth. I panted all the way up the hill, coping with a troublesome digestion that said:

"I told you so, but you just wouldn't listen..."

These coastal villages made for some tough cycling. Their town centres were mostly at the end of a steep descent down to the port and then it was straight up along the other side of the cliff, on roads as steep as a staircase. Luckily, a strong easterly wind kept pushing me as I reached Devon, my fifth county. Remote Dorset had felt at times like an open free campsite, but Devon seemed to be fond of its stout fences. Usually even the tidiest of hedgerows has a hole here and there where one can get into a field, but a good hour out of Exeter I was still unable to find any fault with them.

- Branscombe, DEVON -

Thick bushes everywhere, and barbed wire so tight that even a rabbit would have had trouble trying to squeeze through it. As it was getting seriously dark and late I tried asking. A young couple was out walking their dog and I hoped they would take pity on me and offer a warm meal and a corner of their garden. That didn't quite work out, but they lent a hand with a few phone calls and directions towards a farm campsite where somebody called Martin told them it was a bit late but that he would be waiting for me.

A day later, the cycle route moved on to a disused railway track that cut across the National Park of Dartmoor through a series of long, unlit tunnels. Cyclists were well prepared, but I, too lazy to take out my lights, scared a few of them by ringing my bell in complete darkness. In Tavistock, Brutus experienced his first ever puncture. Once fixed it was all downhill towards Plymouth, through some of the best English countryside, with wild horses roaming freely and gorse bushes in full bloom, smelling of coconut.

Samantha, my host, recommended Harbourside, a fish and chips restaurant, for a change, saying I couldn't possibly miss it.

"It's one of the best in the country." she said .
"In 2018 it was awarded 3rd best in the United Kingdom."

A large sticker on the glass pane commemorated the event, and quality seemed confirmed by the long queue of people patiently waiting for their dinner to be fried perfectly crispy. After months of forced closures, bars, cafés and restaurants had just partially reopened, so long as customers were served outside. The cobbled streets of Sutton Harbour Marina were abuzz with people desperate to finally order a few pints of their favourite beer. I watched the relief on their faces as they stood impervious to the chilly wind, happily raising their glasses with long awaited toasts.

    A short ferry crossing brought me to Mount Edgcumbe. I had set off for this trip on a whim without any expectations or knowledge of what each day would bring. The little boat docked at the pier, and within a few steps a metal signpost told me I was now in Cornwall, and what an entrance it was. The cycleway entered the open gates of what looked like an elegant castle and took me through its vast grounds with open vistas to the ocean and the spectacle of camellias in full bloom. Fish and chips were still prominent in all menus but were now competing with traditional Cornish Pasty. I soon stopped at a place, eager to try my first one. Again it seemed popular with the locals, who kept coming with their cars to collect their take-aways. I asked the cashier what filling she would recommend.

"Have you had *pasty* before?" she asked me.
"A few times, in London, if that counts... Surely not the same..." I replied.

"Not when you are having it from a world champion." was the quick, self-assured answer.

She pointed her finger at a framed plate that hung on the wall and told of some past glories. 2016 it was, and I wasn't sure what had happened since then and if I should ask for an autograph. I was growing suspicious of all these places displaying their awards and setting new records, but I let her decide the filling and sat down on a bench to enjoy it as she stared at me, waiting for praise.

"Wonderful..." I said, ordering a second one.

In truth a hungry cyclist is most forgiving when it comes to food; besides my *pasty* experience was lacking, I certainly couldn't quite tell the difference between a 2016 world champion and the Waterloo Station version I had tasted back in the nineties.

I left and rejoined the coast several times before trying my luck at finding a campsite. As it turned out there were none open. I settled for a grassy forested area not far from Mevagissey, a day away from an old friend who was going to host me for a couple of nights in Penryn. It had been a full week of dry weather and sun, something very rare and un-British. Forecasts promised it would continue, just like the weatherman had predicted, pushing me to start this journey. On board the King Harry ferry I met Robin and a friend; both keen cyclists on light racing bikes, they were members of the Falmouth Wheelers Club. When Robin heard of my nationality he suggested I should follow him to his place for tea, saying he wanted to show me some of his bicycles. I chased him as he sprinted up a few hills like a spring chicken leaving me panting far behind. Over tea and biscuits he told me he was sixty eight years old, which left me rather embarrassed; he also added that he had recently tried to beat the hour world record for his age group, failing by a small margin, which restored some of the lost confidence and made me feel a tad better. We then walked through the garden into a shed where gardening tools had been replaced by a neatly displayed collection of vintage Italian racing bikes like an old Bianchi model I had once owned in my teens.

It was a short ride into Penryn, where Debbie and Chloe were busy moving boxes from their car to the house they had just moved into. Chloe's son is a passionate zoologist and thankfully I was warned from the start that besides the cat and a fish tank I might also bump into reptiles and other exotic residents. There were a few plump geckos and a bearded dragon with an endearing name I couldn't recall. I called it 'the monster'. It was not that large, and I was assured it was absolutely harmless, but it had the looks of a fierce dinosaur. As I walked into the guest room, it was happily crawling about and hiding behind some Ikea cardboard boxes. The pet's feeding habits were as exotic; a hoard of bugs, crickets, grasshoppers and white worms had to be stored alive in their own little boxes before being sacrificed. In the afternoon the search was on for a cricket who, probably aware of its fate, had gone into hiding. His stressful chirp could be heard somewhere between the second and third shelf of a well stocked refrigerator. The rest of the day was spent joining Debbie for a nice walk along the coast and getting acquainted with the reptiles. By the end of it I had even plucked up courage to let the dragon crawl all over my shoulders, immortalising such bravery in a photograph.

I was looking forward to moving on, excited that in a day I would reach Land's End, the southernmost tip of England. I passed the town of Penzance. Here the railway comes to a halt and England pretends to be the French Riviera. Further on was the beautiful oddity that is Minack Theatre, an amphitheatre cast to the side of the idyllic beach of Porthcurno. Rowena Cade, with the help of her trusted gardener Rawlings, built it with her own hands out of love for the theatre. Starting at the end of the First World war, she spent the rest of her life on the project; and her legacy continues, with plays held every summer. Land's End was just around the corner. Sennen Cove was recommended by two local cyclists as the best place to spend a night camping. I sat down on one of the large stones that, like a giant staircase, lead down to a cove and the ocean. The cold meal would have been unremarkable were it not for the half dozen seagulls playing stunts with the wind currents and a view that was priceless. I was woken by the cold night then fell asleep again, my tent clinging to a patch of grass, its walls trembling in the swirling wind. I completed the loop around the tiny peninsula that stretches between Penzance to the South and Saint Ives to the North, arguably the best of Cornwall.

- Sennen Cove, CORNWALL -

The northern coast seemed much quieter, with less tourism and more agriculture. Villages that in the 19th century had been thriving thanks to the tin mines were now derelict and rundown. Every now and then there were more treasures like Hell's Mouth, a little hidden bay with turquoise water and white sand framed by steep cliffs covered with gorse bushes and wild flowers. I pushed the bike along a narrow trail to get the best views and met Tim, a twitcher with a camera lens as long as his forearm. According to him it was all happening there and then, and he expressed his excitement in a live commentary that to me had the authority of a *National Geographic*. I trusted him. If he hadn't been around I would still have enjoyed it but a lot would have gone unnoticed. His remarks sounded like Japanese *haiku*.

"Peregrine Falcon!" he shouted, pointing up at the sky.
"Fastest animal on earth, 300 miles an hour!"

We walked a little further and, as I was still looking up, engrossed in watching such a majestic flight, he pointed not far from my right foot:

"Black Adder! Only poisonous snake in Britain." he said, calmly.

A black serpent was displaying his white geometric patterns, hiding in a thorn bush to the side. I have never been too fond of snakes.

"Shit! That was close!" I said to Tim, having lost some of the initial trust in him and wishing he had warned me a little earlier.

"Oh…Don't worry…" he laughed.
"Remember that they are always more afraid of you than you are of them." he continued, trying to reassure me.

"Not if you step on one they aren't…" I snapped, having lost some of my patience.

He looked at me puzzled, as if despite his wisdom he hadn't thought about that one.

I continued along the trail that led me back to Hell's Mouth, opening into a small car park. In the glorious sunshine I witnessed a peculiarly British habit: the car picnic. I had seen it before in other parts of the country and it never failed to surprise me. It entails driving to a place of outstanding beauty, parking the car and enjoying the picnic safely, behind the windscreen. Usually a thermos flask of afternoon tea and biscuits makes the experience homely and less threatening. Cycling is not always a pleasant activity. There are the inevitable quirks when things do not go quite right and there is nothing one can do about it. After ten glorious days of constant sunshine the weather turned, and I could see the rain coming. My search for a campsite with a hot shower was in vain. Because of the pandemic, campsites in Cornwall were open to campervans only, due to the fact that they could not offer access to basic services. I stopped at quite a few, asking if I could stay, but the refrain was always the same: the toilets are closed and what would I do then? Run to the forest? You bet I would if I had to. I gave up searching and made do with a field outside the village of Cubert. Hardly had I pitched my shelter when it started raining heavily. However, when dry and safe, falling asleep to the sound of raindrops pelting the thin canvas is always a pleasant experience.

Mornings are different, especially if it starts raining when packing up and everything gets wet whilst one is sorting out all the bundles and bags. I scrambled everything together, packing as fast as I could, but it was wet and cold and, for the first time, I felt a hint of sadness. It was relentless and I had to take shelter at a covered bus stop in the centre of the village. I bought a hot coffee at a convenience store, not so much for the taste, but to hold and warm up my hands with it; they felt numb and frozen. A group of students joined me under the roof waiting for the bus, with despondent faces after having woken up too early in order to attend another day of school. We shared that roof for a few minutes, each of us wallowing in his own miseries. In normal times I can face a bad day. I would take a break from cycling, do some sightseeing, have a good rest, or treat myself to a good meal; but right now, none of these were viable options. Being cold and wet when most places were closed, and the few that were open were only offering take-aways, was different. I felt tempted, knowing that London was only a few hours' journey away on a train.

Moods improved and so did the weather. I passed Newquay and Padstow, and eventually found someone willing to take a guest in. Rosina, recently widowed, lived in a large two hundred years old farmhouse. It took me ten minutes to ride the driveway between the gate and the front door. I rang the bell and put a mask on, thinking she might be afraid of catching the bug at her 'not so young' age, but she was full of that British 'no nonsense' attitude and told me to forget about it. She welcomed me in and introduced me to her best friend, a most loving Labrador called Bernie. According to the evening news on the radio, the weather would be improving. I left Roskearn Farm the following morning wishing I could take Bernie with me. I thanked Rosina for the proper shower, the washing machine, the full fat English breakfast and the central heating, and was back to my old chirpy self on the Cornish roads.

I passed the first signposts pointing to the Camel Trail. I thought it an odd name given that I had not seen one yet in Cornwall, but it followed a disused railway track along the Camel river. The old platforms and abandoned stations were well spaced out every few kilometres, while I played at being a train with no carriages. Carpets of bluebells coloured the shady banks. Halfway along the trail it started to drizzle. This time I was better prepared. With a full stomach, thanks to Rosina's bacon and eggs, I put to good use my new rainproof orange poncho, whistling my way through the dripping forest. A few walkers were out and about and were treated to the spectacle of a moving fluorescent tent on wheels. Dogs stopped wagging their tails and looked terrified as I passed them. The Camel trail came to an end, and so did the rain. I removed my poncho and wondered why it had taken me half a century to buy one and stay bone dry on a wet day. I had been told that Cornish is a dead language. All that is left of it are the tongue-twisting names on signposts that nobody quite knows how to pronounce or make any sense of. After the Camel Trail I followed National Cycle Route 3. It took me to the heights of Bodmin Moor's plateau, a pristine nature reserve populated by sheep, cows, dogs and shepherds living in a handful of scattered farms. I had the unusual experience of crossing two long airport runways on a bicycle: 02 and 06 at RAF Davidstow to be precise, once a large Air Force base but nowadays not in use, its taxiways now part of the cycle route.

May was a few days away but I woke up with the tent walls frozen solid as if I had pitched in a high camp on mount Everest. I was back in Devon, back to fighting fences. On a late afternoon I looked for a couple of hours, searching for a few spare square metres, but could not find anything. Everywhere just sheep and cows guarded by copious barbed wire. It got too late again and without being too picky I settled for a grassy lot behind the first ever broken fence. It was clearly land belonging to one of the two houses that I could see on either side, still it was too late to be fussy and with the help of the fading light I gambled. At night time I realised that putting my inflatable mattress next to Rosina's hot heater had not been a smart move. The heat had obviously messed up the thin material and as I was inflating it, it started popping and then exploded, leaving a sizeable hole. That made the night a little colder and the back sorer from the gnarly ground. Not to risk meeting the farmer I had to pack up and leave by six, in arctic temperatures and just before sunrise. Later in Bideford I mentioned my experience to a fisherman whose life had taught him how to keep comfortable at night in a fishing boat; he seemed to know a thing or two about inflatable mattresses and as soon as I mentioned the explosion he immediately asked:

"You put it on a heater, didn't you?"

As I nodded, surprised by the accurate guess, he covered his face with both hands and then raised his eyes to the sky, all clear signs that I should not have done it. Another flat, disused railway track with an exotic name awaited me, the Tarka Trail to Barnstaple. Lovely as it was I had first to deal with frostbite on my hands despite the winter gloves I was wearing. It was all put into perspective by a couple of purple joggers running in shorts and thin lycra on frosty ground at seven in the morning.

    After the sunny start, it clouded over just as I began climbing the hills of Exmoor National Park. The Dutch poncho came back into use. Thoroughly miserable, I pushed the bike up a steep road in pelting hail. Clouds were dark, gloomy and hopeless but every now and then the sun broke through in some clear patches. Before exiting the National Park the sky turned threatening once again, so I thought it best to pick a nice spot early. It was a cold but lovely night up on Exmoor. I shared the space with running rabbits and two cuckoos having a repetitive conversation. The following day I descended the hills, reaching the lovely village of Dulverton and crossing into Somerset, which was to be my last county. With the sun shining on the Exmoor greens as a backdrop, it looked like a village out of a fairytale; everyone seemed happy and followed a strict policy of greeting even a stranger like me with a 'good morning!' Next was Bampton, winner of 'Best village in bloom' in 1989, before letting standards slip a little. Two weeks of cold and a year long lockdown brought out the mischievous side of me. I hadn't planned it. It all happened impulsively as I was exiting the village. I stopped right outside a house by a large field with a sign saying Bampton South Scouts. Not sure of the right direction, I leaned the bike against the wall and was looking at a map on my phone when two men by the gate approached me and asked what I was looking for.

"Bampton Scouts North" I said, joking but trying to look serious.

"This is it! Bampton Scouts South." one of them replied.

"You are not Malcolm by any chance, are you?" I asked, hoping neither of them would bear such a name.

"No...I don't think there's any Malcolm as far as I know..."

"I am pretty sure it was North..." I said with conviction. Let me find out." Moving back to where the bike was, I faked a short phone conversation.

"Eddie, I made it to Bampton but they only seem to have a Bampton Scouts South. Is that the one?"
"Oh...I see. I was pretty sure it was North. Ok...I will keep going then..."
"Many thanks." I said to the two of them
"I need to move on...It looks like I have got the wrong side of the village."

I waved goodbye and continued, wondering what the two made of it. Was a Bampton North covert group plotting to take over their territory?

Trivia: in Somerset, horse poo was then trading at £1.50 per bag or 15 pence per kilo. You could have a five bags deal for a fiver. Not that I wanted or needed one.

The first half of the day was spent on cycleways while for the second half I moved to bigger roads in order to make it all the way to Glastonbury. What a strange and peculiar place. A small village that for a few days a year becomes the centre of the world and is flooded with hundreds of thousands of city dwellers, coming for rock and roll, beer and plenty of mud. It was definitely quiet and off-season. After buying food supplies in the High Street I found a kind farmer tilling his soil on a huge tractor. I asked if I could put the tent somewhere and he pointed to the field across the road and was even polite enough to ask me for how many nights.

Early the following morning I got to appreciate the other side of Glastonbury's fame as I stopped in the village for breakfast. It is also well known as the capital of New Age and Neopagan beliefs and as the spring of all kinds of cults. Reading up about it, I discovered that it had all started due to its links with myths and legends related to the Holy Grail, King Arthur and Joseph of Arimathea. Religion was on sale in all its flavours, shapes and forms. The entire economy of the little town seemed based around it. While it was really hard to find a good meal or a decent cup of coffee, it was perfect if you were after a particular brand of incense, or bells, singing bowls and chimes, or amulets to guard against the worst misfortune. There were clinics offering all kinds of weird services. There were 'soul therapists', and a shop owned by a self-professed Maitreya, the Buddha of the future, conveniently reborn near the M5 motorway. There were Druid and Celtic cults and more exotic fads that seemed to have landed from some distant planets. For thirty five pounds, which I thought was quite a bargain, you could meditate under an ascension pyramid. For the more well off and spiritually advanced there was a 'Etheric Weaver treatment on a Metatron Mat'. I wondered what it might do to one, hopefully not too much harm.

Disappointed and unenlightened I left for Wells. It advertised itself humbly, as the smallest city in England, but its charm and beauty was a real surprise. I would say it was one of the nicest towns I have ever visited in the country, and for some strange reason I had never even heard of it. Some of its elegance was thanks to it being the residence of the Bishops of Bath and Wells. The large close surrounding the cathedral was a real gem cast in the town centre, open for people to walk around and enjoy. Next on the agenda was Bath itself, my final destination. It was reached via another disused railway track that took me through the longest tunnel I had ever cycled. One and a half miles long, Combe Down Tunnel enveloped me in its darkness for six long minutes. Halfway through I realised it was particularly dark as I had forgotten to take off my sunglasses. I had originally planned to take three more days to reach my starting point in London, but some stormy weather was on the way and enough cold had already been endured. I thought it best to call it a day and end on a good note, being satisfied with what I had seen and what I had done.

- Wells, SOMERSET -

Scottish Highlands

Scottish Highlands

With international travel still limited, I decided to trade some good, summery weather for a change of scenery. Relatively close, Scotland had often been on people's lips when asking for cycling recommendations; some considered it unmissable. The inevitable closing phrase went something like: "It's wonderful...if you get good weather...", said with a hint of sadness that convinced me they must have had plenty of rain. For this reason I had been procrastinating, convinced it was the kind of place best visited in a 4x4 vehicle, with wellies and large umbrellas. The pandemic neatly arranged things for me and I felt grateful. Stuck in the British Isles, a bike ride in the Scottish Highlands seemed full of appeal and as exotic as it gets. After all, I recalled meeting a couple of Germans in Patagonia; they had travelled halfway around the world to get there and told me that the landscape reminded them of Scotland.

A short flight brought me from the congestion of London to the silence of Inverness airport. The views over lochs and firths, forests and moorland was a *deja vu* of the landing in Balmaceda, Chile. There were the same strong gusts of wind and the same limited signs of human presence in the few white strips of roads criss-crossing the landscape. On my way to the west coast I had to cross Inverness city centre, where I succeeded in finding a tiny Scottish flag to patch to my hat; an effort to persuade the locals to be more friendly. Within half an hour the pale sun that had welcomed my arrival disappeared and, as I was leaving the city, grey clouds gathered in earnest and got darker and darker before settling into a steady drizzle. I took cover under the large roof of a petrol station, donning my fluorescent orange poncho, determined to keep going. In the eyes of the Scots I was surely overdoing it, and as a couple passed me to get into the café I could tell they were a little bemused and probably wondering what I would do when it started to rain properly. Once I reached the suburbs traffic got thinner and I noticed the first signs pointing to the start of the North Coast 500. It had been marketed as nothing less than one of the most epic routes in the world, a kind of Route 66 for the Scottish. Its popularity was a recent phenomenon, the result of a publicity campaign aimed at boosting tourism in the Highlands or, more cynically, to get cyclists and motorbikers from around the world extremely wet and soggy. The route in fact promised to take the wannabe adventurer in a loop around one of the wettest coasts on Earth all the way up to John O'Groats before allowing one to dry off a little, heading South along the eastern coast and back into Inverness.

- Inverness, SCOTLAND -

The abrupt introduction to the local weather continued on and off for the rest of the day until I spotted a hideout by the side of the road, just in time before the next downpour. It was a round patch of moss encircled by a thick forest: not perfect, but it was not the time to be fussy. It was there that I had my first encounter with the dreaded midges, one of Scotlands' main summer drawbacks and a strong natural deterrent against camping. These blighters, despite their minute size, are known to be capable of reducing grown men to tears. I had done my homework and arrived ready to fight them with a mix of citronella flavoured spray and a head net that made me look like a cross between a beekeeper and a bank robber.

The Scots, in their resourcefulness and determination to survive them, have come up with a mobile phone App; it is called Smidgeometer and warns one, with some accuracy, when it is time to stop cursing and use lots of spray instead. I hadn't noticed their presence as I stopped but while trampling on the soft ground clouds of them started pestering me. I had a quick glance at the App; we were just at beginner level, two out of five. It did not reassure me, let alone make me feel any better. The bugs couldn't believe their luck: someone was attempting to put up a tent in their midst on an otherwise dreadful and wet day. I donned the dreadful head net and erected the tent as fast as I could, taking cover inside it; the little bastards stared at me, unable to squeeze through the finest netting they had ever seen. I liked the spray, it had a nice fragrance that seemed most effective because they soon lost interest in me. Ten pounds well spent. The only drawback was that one had to put it on every inch of exposed skin and on the face, and it left a bitter aftertaste to anything I ate. I doubt there is much space left for a brain cell in there yet the little rascals are smart, with the sharpest survival instinct. They somehow know that a grown up man out camping will inevitably have to exit his tent for a pee and by then he or she will have completely forgotten about health and safety. They patiently sat and waited on the roof ready to get me, and they did. Peeing in nature never felt less appealing and had to be done in a hurry. I tried to master the art of zipping and unzipping trousers and tent doors quickly but a few inevitably managed to sneak in and had to be squashed, mercilessly.

The following day started sunny, then clouds gathered out of nowhere and it started pouring, seeping through anything that wasn't made of Gore-tex. Ahead was Bealach na Ba, the mountain that according to some cyclists was the toughest ride in the entire country. A couple of youngsters on racing bikes overtook me and, staring at my bike and loaded bags, wondered aloud if I would ever make it. The weather was not on my side, but the climb didn't look too bad to start with. The tarmac climbed gently in a couple of hairpin turns before revealing a seriously steep straight where gale force winds started blowing full against me. Dark clouds billowed high in the sky, morphing into threatening shapes, with a few patches of deep blue sky that made it all the more dramatic. Halfway up I was clinging for life to the handlebars and to the mountain, trying not to get blown back down to where I had started. Never had I cycled so slowly, suffering pedal stroke after pedal stroke in a balancing act to remain upright. It felt like hopelessly cycling in one of the hells of Dante. After a couple of hours, I reached the top in anguish. Balach na Ba was indeed the hardest climb in the country. The wind continued blustery as I started the descent down the other side towards Applecross' campsite.

From Applecross the twisty road turned into a single track that headed north, first sticking to the edge of the west coast and then along a wide valley, uninhabited beyond a handful of farms. Above me was a blue sky with scattered, fast moving clouds, low enough to be caught in outstretched arms. The observations of others made much more sense now. Had I been dropped here blindfolded, I might as well have guessed being back in Patagonia; and the white mountains, covered in snow even in mid-summer, seemed a miniature replica of the mighty Andes. In the Highlands too, as in South America, a single derelict house qualifies as a village and is given a proper name. Similarly, facilities are sparse and, given all the rain, there is a remarkable lack of roofs to take shelter under. Forecasts, of course, are best taken with a pinch of salt. With the ever present strong winds and the nearby Atlantic Ocean, predicting the weather correctly has similar odds to winning the jackpot in a lottery.

At times the smell of the rain merged with the salty taste of the sea as I caught glimpses of the rugged Hebrides not too far across the narrow straight. Unlike Portsmouth, gorse flowers really smelled of coconut, as did my shampoo; at my worst, when feeling sad and wet, I dreamt of the tropics and of kinder climates. I followed the road to Loch Torridon where a stretched finger of land reaches the fishing port of Shieldaig. Beyond that, I left the coast and turned inland, following the river Torridon along a vast prairie and the rising slopes of Beinn Heige. My final destination for the day was Kinnlochewe. Having a few times attempted to ask for directions, my pronunciation drew only giggles or blank faces. I thought it should be something like Kim Law Chew even if it sounded like a Chinese take-away. As it turned out there was a disguised 'loch' in the name, resulting in 'Keen Loch Hugh'. I finally reached it, having learnt to pronounce it correctly.

I arrived at the campsite and discovered that the owner had devised an original check-in system that started at five pm and guaranteed a glorious gridlock outside the gate. I joined the longish queue for about thirty minutes to start with. Once it was my turn I realised that the excessive wait was also compounded by further complications developed by the owner as a way to keep people distanced during the ongoing pandemic. It involved plastic loops of different colours that had to be left hanging on specific hooks in common areas so that the number of people accessing them could be controlled. Green loops were for toilets while red loops meant laundry and yellow ones were for the kitchen area. No loops outside a door hook meant full capacity had been reached; in reality often people just shoved them in their pockets and forgot all about the ingenious system. Unnecessary queues developed outside public facilities while guests walked around the property in deep thought, colourful loops dangling from their fingers as they tried to remember where they had picked them up and on which hook they belonged. A guidebook with further details would have come in handy but our host hadn't yet found the time to write it and in the meantime seemed to be enjoying the confusion that ensued. The Smidgeometer's readings shot up to a critical level four by early evening. Loops and hooks, while still problematic, were the least of my worries. Campers keen to experience the Scottish outdoors, walked about the campsite to the sound of slapping hands on arms and legs. Something didn't feel quite right about adults having polite conversations with their faces covered in brownish head nets. With some relief I noticed that midges, once they managed to get into the tent, behaved admirably. Unlike mosquitoes that come at you relentlessly, they happily clung to the tent's roof as if hypnotised and stayed put. Movement is what excited them and they were back to swarming around me by the morning as I dismantled my camp. I am all for animal welfare when animals play their part and contribute something to the environment, but midges' only seem to exist to make a misery of well deserved summer holidays. Once moving on the bike they disappeared, limited by their average flying speed, which I read was only three kilometres per hour, thankfully slower than I was travelling.

The weather on the west coast became glorious, with just a couple of brief drizzles per day. I cycled around Beinn Heige which, as is the case for mountains over one thousand metres, is given the title of 'Munro'. The road turned into a well surfaced two lanes, with a little more traffic and a few dicey overtaking manoeuvres as cars passed me. I rejoined the coast at Poolewe where a grand vista opened suddenly on to the sea. A few days after the previous encounter, I crossed paths again with one of the lads I had briefly chatted to at the foot of Bealach na Ba. The chap, who previously had glanced at my bike and said "you are not doing it on that, are you?" had in the meantime overdone it on the climb, pulling a leg muscle; I subsequently heard he had to give up the ride entirely, taking a bus back to Bolton….I smiled to myself, thinking that it must have been a case of prompt and fair *karma* retribution.

- Ardvreck Castle, SCOTLAND -

I checked in at the beachside campsite in Laide. It was a classic night of European football with a scheduled match between Scotland and England. I asked if there was somewhere I could watch it but the virus forbade unnecessary assembling and, extraordinarily, this also applied to football. The campervans locked their doors shut and tuned their satellite dishes and televisions sets, while I thought I would guess the score by gauging the levels of shouting. Two hours passed in a total silence that told the story of a boring match that ended in a goalless tie.

As already mentioned, the local twists to the language made it impossible to pronounce town names correctly, but I was unexpectedly helped by having a foreign accent myself. Scottish people made an effort to speak more clearly out of a kindness that was not always granted to the English; an elderly couple from Hampshire told me they were struggling, having serious difficulties communicating. The further north I travelled the more the weather turned stroppy and angry. Rain fell in buckets as I descended the mountain valley along Glen More: I was enveloped in a misty grey soup, a black and white landscape in which the only colours were the lilac rhododendron bushes in full bloom. Sixty wet kilometres with neither a roof nor a café. Once I reached the village of Ullapool, I sat out the rain biding my time at the local Fish and Chips shop while getting rid of some dampness. The plan worked to some extent, and I felt able to continue all the way to Ardmair Point and another busy campsite.

The last decade has seen a shift in the corporate world's favourite pastime. High flyers who once used their little spare time to hit balls at golf courses have more recently turned into keen cyclists. With bikes that are feather weight but can cost as much as a budget car, the more competitive types have moved their interest from birdies and eagles to excruciatingly long rides. I had just settled in at the campsite and was enjoying an ice-cream outside the reception café when Alistair limped in exhausted, on a flashy titanium racing bike that I would have needed a mortgage to buy. He stopped in front of the lowered barrier and screamed a loud "for f*** sake". I went up to him to find out what had happened and realised that there was a sign that said 'campsite full'.

"You look tired." I said jokingly.

"Don't worry too much about the sign," I told him, "they'll let you in if you tell them you are cycling."

My news cheered him up a little before he started complaining about calf pain and of having cycled too long on that day.

"I shouldn't have pushed it that far..." he said, and I agreed with him when I figured out he had covered, in a single day, what had taken me three rather enjoyable days.

At five in the morning I got up for a toilet call and there was no sign of Alistair's tent. He had obviously not learnt his lesson yet and had set off far too early for another long grind.

 Well aware that the following few days would be the highlight of the entire journey, I prayed for merciful weather and my request was granted. Initially forecasts were rather dicey. The morning started out cloudy but as I moved closer to Lochinver the sky broke open, uncovering some hopeful blue patches. I swerved left onto the smaller road I could take, a longer diversion that rewards in views by hugging the coastline. Wide enough to accommodate two lanes to start with, it soon turned into a narrow single track with a few side spots here and there to allow cars to pass. Good vistas were consistent and most impressive, reaching their climax in the little paradise of Achmelvich, which I reached on the first day of summer. If it wasn't for the fresh temperatures and the blistering winds, the white sandy beach and the turquoise waters gave me the illusion of being in the Maldives or the Bahamas. There was a campsite to one side of the peninsula where I had planned to stay but it was only allowing campervans. For the first time in my life of cycling, the receptionist was unwavering and travelling on a bicycle was not a good enough excuse. It turned out to be my best luck. Scotland has a 'right to roam' rule that allows free camping on public land provided one moves on the next day. The guy at the campsite reminded me of my rights, telling me I could camp pretty much wherever I wanted outside the campsite gates. I pushed the bike up, along a path with large boulders and patches of grass perfectly trimmed, like the green of a fancy golf course. I could pick and choose the spot that was most picture perfect and settled for one right on top of the beach, a hundred feet above the ocean.

I left Achmelvich in the sun, as I had found it. I started a relentless progress up and down hills that lasted for about an hour, enough time for clouds to gather from nowhere and for rain to fall without mercy. After a quick descent to Clachtoll it was again back to how I liked it, and I was bathing in sunshine. Lambs roamed free all over the place, often crossing the road in search for better grazing. Reaching Loch Glencoul the single track merged with a larger road and opened up to more outstanding views of the sea and steep slopes covered with green fern. I found a tiny café with freshly baked cakes where I heard French being spoken. Years back, a young couple had come here on holiday and fallen in love with the place; they swapped their little village in the Alps to an even smaller one in the Highlands. I thought they must enjoy solitude and silence but as I sat there indulging in a collection of sweets and pies, people trickled in from nowhere, on a pilgrimage in search of strong coffee and delicious cakes. Halfway through a day of cycling, rhododendrons replaced the heather and the lilac tints that had accompanied my journey turned magenta, adding to the yellows of gorse.

    The summer solstice brought the stretched out days of the North, where the sun rises at four o'clock in the morning and does not set before ten thirty. I wondered how different these places must look in winter when only little light is granted. To get through long months of cold, rain and darkness, one probably needs all that good whisky, if not a regular prescription of antidepressants. From Scourie to Durness to the Kyle of Tongue, the wilderness was once more at its grandest. I cycled through land that reminded me of the vast plains I had seen in Canada or the US but that are so rare in Europe. Beyond Durness were Sango and Highland Bay, yet again the coast at its best with more stunning alcoves of white sand and a sea to rival exclusive resorts found far away in the tropics. Hardly anybody was brave enough to take a dip in the water. The road took me in a three quarter loop around Loch Eriboll, where I kept a thin slit of sea to one side and gently rising mountains to the other. Strong winds pushed me, making good progress painless and much faster.

Just before reaching Kyle of Tongue it started to drizzle, but I managed to pitch my tent in the middle of an empty grass field on what seemed a quiet and empty rural campsite. It was late evening but there were only a handful of campervans and a couple of tents around me. All seemed happy to sit out the rain and have a peaceful rest, but things were about to get spicy. Just past nine in the evening I covered my eyes to block out the lingering daylight and put in some earplugs just to be on the safe side. Half an hour passed in total silence, at which point a roar of cars and motorbikes revving their engines got louder and louder echoing in the valley.

    Next a hustle and bustle started all around me, in what I assumed was a hopeless effort to pitch a tent while keeping dry in the pouring rain. It got noisier, it sounded quite a crowd. Each conversation was belted out with full lungs like a tenor reaching the climax of *Nessun Dorma*, which coincidentally, means nobody should sleep in Italian. There was more huffing and puffing and some cursing about the poor weather in a mix of English and what sounded like a foreign language. There were certainly plenty of tent pegs to be hammered in, so many that I couldn't help but wonder whether they were setting up a circus or something of that kind. The hammering got too close for comfort. I unzipped my tent and could not believe my eyes. An army-sized tent was rising tall, hardly half a metre away from mine. To give it any chance of standing, it needed a complicated set of criss-crossing ropes and guidelines; some passed right over one side of my tent and looped around it in an obviously rushed job where safety, distances and measurements had been badly misjudged. Annoyed by the late night noise and lack of consideration I thought I should say something.

"Don't you think your 'tent' is a little too close to mine?"

"...and what about all these strings?"

"I could trip and kill myself going for a pee at night!"

They all stopped hammering and stared at me, surprised by my claims which in fairness were a little over dramatic. It was a group of either Indians or Pakistanis, and certainly not the traditional campers one expects in the remoteness of the Scottish Highlands. They turned out to be most polite. One of them walked closer and apologised, even though he probably could not quite tell what was wrong with it.

"Sorry," he said, "we thought your tent door was on the other side."

Once I returned to my tent more hammering promptly restarted. By eleven I could hear a large bonfire making a crackling sound. I unzipped the tent as plumes of smoke engulfed the entire campsite. Were they now trying to set alight the place? A man in a campervan not far from me was looking through the slit of his open door before locking it up, hoping things would be alright. Close to midnight the mother of all barbecues started. The scent of grilled meat pervaded the valley and when it was cooked to perfection a looping series of calls started:

"Lamb chops are ready!"
"Who wants a lamb chop?"
"Come on! There's plenty of food here!"

Then the chicken was ready…

"Chicken thighs now ready!"
"Anybody for chicken thighs?"
"Come on Abdul, you don't like chicken thighs?! Why don't you have a lamb chop?"

Just as I was about to storm out of my tent for the second time with something like:
"For God's sake, people are trying to sleep here…and by the way, I haven't had a bloody lamb chop!", the voice of a lady started calling outside my door.

"Hello sir, anybody there?"
"Sir…would you like a lamb chop?"

I had eaten dinner five hours before, but with not much chance of getting any sleep I thought I might as well join them and find out what all these celebrations were about.

"You bet, I want one!" I snapped.

"I bring it here?" she said.

"No, you are not doing that! I will come there and join the olympic barbecue."

By now a large yurt that really looked like a mini circus, had also been erected next to the humongous tent I had seen earlier, and to one side were another two good-sized tents. No wonder all the hammering. It reminded me of the nomad's camps I had spent the night at on the high plains of Central Asia or an UNHCR emergency camp after some kind of natural tragedy.

A large gazebo, extending out from one side of a van, had been set up as a fully functioning kitchen fuelled by large gas canisters. At the centre of it, larger than life, was Habib, a long bearded man in a white tunic who was clearly in charge; he showed it by holding an extra large metal fork in one hand and a heavy duty butcher's knife in the other. He looked happy and proud and in total control of three large barbecues filled with sizzling meats in all kinds of marinades and spices. No one was allowed to get too close.

"Sit down." He commanded me.

"Here. Take a lamb chop."

"Who else wants a lamb chop?"

"Abdul! Why don't you have another lamb chop!"

I found out they were originally from Kashmir, but lived around Manchester and other towns and cities, mostly in northern England. Habib complained about the virus with some sadness saying how, because of it, this year they were only eighteen.

"Last year was much better," he said, "we were twenty-eight."

"Mostly family…" he was quick to point out.

That probably meant another couple of tents, and I was happy to have missed that. In what was by now a family tradition, they reserved a week in summer to reunite somewhere in the Scottish Highlands, in order to be merry, eat plenty of lamb and keep their neighbours awake at night. Given the amount of kerfuffle and planning involved in setting up all their gear, I assumed that they would stay put for at least a week, but that would have been far too easy. They moved daily, Habib told me, and stayed in a different campsite each night. Whether they were doing so voluntarily or were forcibly removed from each one was not clear.

"You do this every night?" I asked him, incredulous.

"Almost." said Habib with some pride.

"Have another lamb chop."

"By the way…where do you get all this lamb from?" I asked him, wondering about the logistics of carrying such quantities of meat in a non-refrigerated van.

He sounded a bit surprised by the question and gave an elusive answer.

"Oh… there's plenty of meat around here!" he said while turning and pointing his large fork towards the mountains.

It was about two o'clock at night when either the meat ran out or they couldn't stomach any more of it. Peace descended on the valley, as I tried to get more sleep with a stomach that felt unusually heavy.

I couldn't really complain too much about the weather so far. However, after the Kashmiri night, it turned bad with a vengeance, making for some heroic cycling, a need to stay positive and keep good manners. It was the perfect mix of a cyclist's worst fears; blistering cold temperatures, a rain that drenched me most of the day and a fierce headwind blowing right into my face. Nevertheless I made it to John O'Groats, the northernmost point in Britain, after having cycled to the southernmost tip, Land's End, only a couple of months before.

The pictures I took in front of the famous signposts pointing to opposite corners of the Earth were soggy and told the whole story. In Land's End it had been sunny and I was smiling. Here I asked a young chap to quickly snap me a souvenir while shaking with a dampness that seeped right to the bones. Black clouds were hanging so low that I could almost touch them. I reached Wick and headed straight for a hot meal at a local restaurant. I fixed my bike to a lamp post and slowly opened the door dripping wet, asking permission to sit down in such a sorry state.

"Is this alright? Sorry, I am a bit wet…" I said in an understatement.

I had forgotten that this being Scotland, they were not in the least surprised and knew exactly what customers most wanted. The waitress disappeared briefly then returned and handed me a large bath towel before showing me the way to a window table. It was all done so naturally that it seemed just part of the regular service. I wasn't alone. Most customers in fact walked in dripping and had their own towels served promptly. In fact hardly anyone bothered carrying an umbrella around Wick. I suppose with the gale force winds and a rain that comes at you in 3D, umbrellas simply don't cut the ice, and so people just learn to face up to it.

- Durness, SCOTLAND -

I had expected the last three days back to Inverness to be less than exciting, especially after the majestic scenery of the previous week. The weather didn't help, but also the mountains disappeared and were replaced by gently rolling hills and farmland that seemed rather ordinary. After another day in the rain I took cover under my tent at a campsite in Dunbeath. I asked the owner whether I could get access to a tumble dryer. The owner apologised and told me that for some ecological reasons he was against them; it struck me as odd in a country where keeping clothes dry increases chances of survival. He showed me to a messy boiler room instead, where a few rope lines were hanging between the walls and the temperature was mild and balmy. I washed and hung my clothes there, and waited sitting in a corner to warm up a little and to dry my soul.

The final stretch to Inverness followed one of the main roads along the eastern coast. In some parts it reminded me of the beloved landscapes around Big Sur, where grass green slopes disappear suddenly, falling steeply into the ocean. A few times I bumped into a cyclist called Martin. A retired man from Sussex, he had left home a month earlier on his bicycle and was now beginning his return journey back South. We had first met the day before at the campsite where at three in the morning I realised that his tent, that had been set up right next to mine, had vanished. I thought it was a bit odd and wondered whether he was a night cyclist. Meeting him again I asked him what had happened. He said he was wary of a group of Geordie lads that had arrived that evening in a van, as he was sure they were going to have a noisy party. Despite having paid his fee, at night he picked up his bike and tent and moved to a field nearby. It made me laugh as it reminded me of the 'Kashmiri lamb chop party' I had endured.

The only advantage of dreadful weather was that the midges had completely disappeared, blown into some Arctic oblivion by the strong southwesterly winds.
However, once the rain and the wind had calmed down they reappeared and we were back at level two. The most common Scottish summer phrase returned to people's lips: "F***ing midges", always preceded by a slapping sound on flesh. My last memorable Scottish experience happened the following morning as I stopped to check my maps in a tiny village. I thought it must have been all that rain and that I was hallucinating. My eyes glanced to one side where I detected some movement; a few metres away behind an ancient red telephone box I spotted the horns and large eyes of a deer looking straight at me.

The North Coast 500 then merged with National Cycle Route 1 which is the traditional way to ride from the top to the bottom of this island. I was hoping to get a celebratory taste of Scotch whisky at Glenmorangie distillery, but I arrived too early and it was still closed. A little further on, I crossed the path of another cyclist, who shouted at me to stop.

"Are you the guy that travels on a Brompton?" he asked me.
The question seemed odd, as I obviously was, but I knew what he meant.

"I am Michael. I have watched all your videos. You are a legend!" he told me.

I felt a little puffed up, but fame was cut short:

"I wrote to you just a few weeks ago about the First Aid kit… remember?"

I did. I recalled he had taken issue with a video tutorial where I packed a first aid kit at the bottom of my rucksack. First aid should always be on top, he had remarked with an exclamation mark. When you badly need it, it should be the easiest thing to reach. A bit pedantic I thought at the time, but he was right. After meeting him he turned out to be a really nice and friendly chap. I apologised in advance to him, admitting that on this particular trip I was not even carrying one, relying entirely on ambulances, paramedics and the wonder of the NHS. He was on the last couple of days of a Land's End to John O'Groats trip, on a bigger touring bike and, given his generous size, I thought he was the real legend and not me.

I believe all trips should ideally end with a majestic bridge crossing over the sea. After the Golden Gate in San Francisco and the Lions Gate of Vancouver it was the turn of Kessock Bridge from where I stared at the last grand views before moving back into Inverness where it had all started.

 What do I think about Scotland?

It's beautiful… if you get good weather… and mind the midges.

* * *

Sicily's South

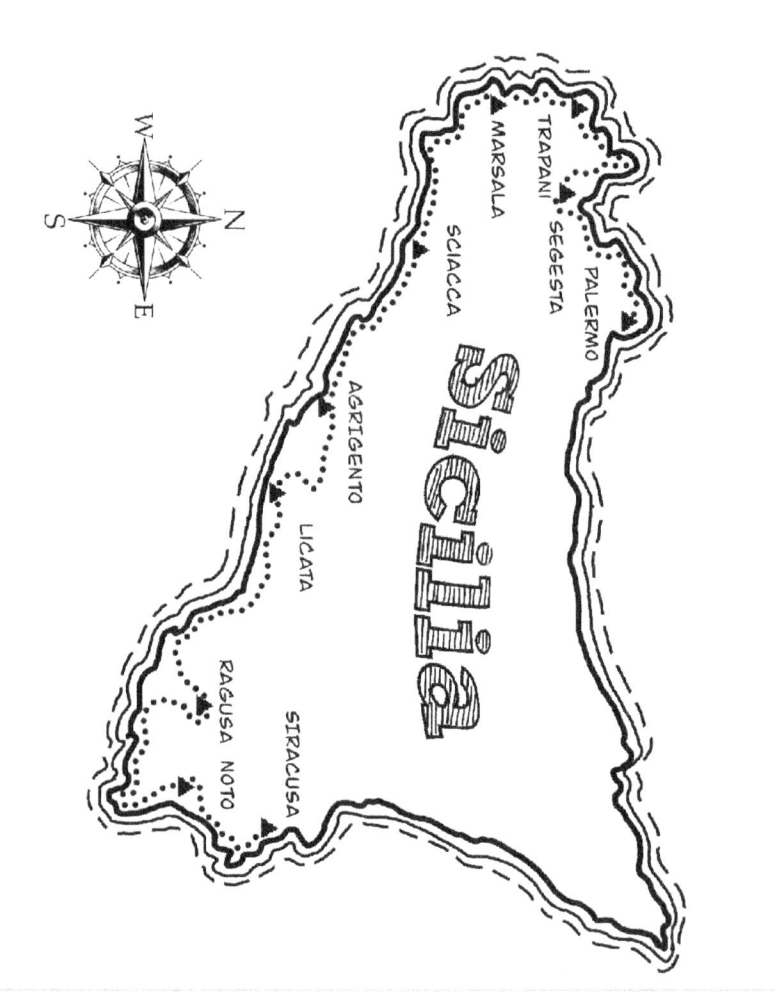

Sicily's South

I had briefly been to Sicily as a teenager, spending a few days playing a tennis tournament in Palermo, so I had hardly done it justice. The idea of returning one day had never really left me, as I had no doubt that it deserved a lot more time, ideally on a bicycle. Fast forward half a lifetime and I found myself approaching Punta Raisi, a flat corner squashed between the sea and the mountains and a challenging runway for planes to land on. I looked down to where the dark blues of the deep sea changed to the pistachio greens of the shallow coastline. A bunch of tiny islets appeared, looking like splattered dots on a glistening canvas. A little further out on the horizon were the reflecting lights of a Palermo sunset, with dramatic peaks rising steeply behind it, as if standing guard. Interesting though it would have been, I preferred to miss the chaos of a busy city and to begin my cycling tour along the southern perimeter, on the opposite side of the island.

The following day the weather played all its tricks on me, shifting gear from a sunny hot start into a full storm with thunder and lightning. Just my bad luck to encounter fluke rainfall in a land plagued by droughts; it was the end of September and I got soaked and unexpectedly chilly in my light clothes. By the time I reached Castellammare del Golfo the clouds were slowly parting and the rain eventually stopped. The campsites shown further along the road on my map turned out to be closed. Later I heard how three years earlier the local river had flooded, sending their guests running for their lives. Incredibly nobody had died then, but the owners' permits had since been revoked. I backtracked to Castellammare, reaching it as it started to get dark, and pitched my tent as if blindfolded.

When I woke up in the morning I realised that my tent was not far from those of three other cyclists. Lorenzo, a Tuscan who was living in Rome, was one of them. One day, into his forties and quite out of the blue, he had decided it was about time to set off on a bike tour. I met him as he was dismantling his tent after his first ever night of camping. He was wondering how on earth he could put all his stuff back into the two panniers he had taken it out from only the night before. It was a complicated puzzle; and then there were the clothes that had not dried properly, which he was wondering what to do with. I had been there myself when I started touring, a necessary rite of passage. More rain was forecast for that afternoon so I decided to stay local, enjoying a day's ride up the mountains and a visit to the Greek temple of Segesta.

- Segesta, SICILY -

As it turned out, a hazy sun was shining as I pedalled up the hills on a winding road smelling the sour scent of prickly pears that were hanging ripe on the large cacti plants. I had almost reached the top when I caught my first views of the temple that has been dominating the landscape for over two thousand five hundred years. It was a humbling thought and I felt privileged to be able to spend even a little time in such a magic place. As the road ended I leaned Brutus to one side of the ticket office and continued on foot, following the trails all the way to the ancient amphitheatre where opera performances and concerts are still staged throughout the summer. On the way down I stopped and sat down at a fruit stall to take in the grand views and enjoy a few slices of the sweetest melon. The lady at the stall didn't miss her chance when I mentioned never having tasted prickly pears. There were orange ones and white ones, all of them sweet and tender but with a mellow and uninspiring taste. Before I knew it, several varieties were served on a plastic plate in front of me.

Talking of plastic, as I descended back to the coast on a quieter road I first encountered a well known problem that has plagued this island since time immemorial: 'waste management' or rather the lack of it. I had been warned that it was part of the 'experience' and that there were epic amounts of it; plastic bottles, cans and rubbish bags had been dumped by the roadside as if fly tipping was a favourite pastime. It was in such stark contrast to the beautiful surroundings that I couldn't help feeling sad and upset about it. During a break I had a chat with a young couple from Palermo and, without me mentioning it, they started telling me how ashamed they felt and how much they shared my feelings. Sicilians don't deserve such a beautiful land, they told me. It gave me some hope that one day things will change and that new generations will finally put an end to it.

It is no secret that Sicilian regional authorities and their administrations have historically been incompetent, at times corrupt, and regularly found wanting. A classic example, and an often quoted one, is that of the island's Forestry. Its staff vastly outnumbers the personnel who look after the entire Alpine range, with a total number short of twenty thousand, half the tally for the entire country. Secure and guaranteed for a lifetime, it is the perfect career for any Sicilian with good connections and acquaintances in the right places. Their main duty is managing the forests in order to prevent wildfires in summer, but there is a consensus that their main task is actually to justify the need for such a vast workforce and that most fires are actually started by themselves in the first place! Beppino, the elderly owner of the campsite at Castellana was convinced of this:

"In the past, mountain lands were managed by shepherds." he told me.

"They knew exactly what had to be done and there was hardly any trouble."

"Then this lot was put in charge" he continued shrugging his shoulders, "and the place is punctually ablaze, every summer."

He was a minute man, at a guess in his seventies. Officially retired, he sat peacefully all day in a wooden armchair, overlooking the reception's veranda. He was keen to point out that despite his age he was as busy as ever, mostly keeping an eye on his son Vincenzo, who had recently been tasked to manage the campsite.
Still there was no doubt as to who was really in charge. Beppino directed operations silently, using a secret code made up of icy stares and the raising or lowering of his eyebrows. When guests approached the son with tricky questions, or whenever something important had to be decided, Vincenzo simply glanced sideways at him and got the right answer. There were rare times when his father spoke and it was usually a *"nu saccie..."*, "I haven't got a clue" in Sicilian dialect. When that happened they both shrugged their shoulders and the guests had to wait patiently for a God- given answer. Each time Vincenzo said something to me it was a reminder that I was a foreigner in my own country. He knew where I was from, that I had been born in a part of Italy that, to him, might as well have been Germany. Because of this,

he made some effort to enunciate his Italian language as clearly as possible, but his exotic accent often tricked me.

"What?" I usually answered, clueless, prompting him to patiently repeat it more slowly so that I would get the gist of it.

I asked him about the prickly pears, eager to know if I could partake in the bounty that was ripe by the roadside rather than buying them. To my surprise he said he had never picked one and warned me that their invisible thorns can cause sizeable wounds.

"They dig into your hands as you try to peel them."
"Better left to the experts..." he told me.

He went on, talking about constipation and that eating the wrong type at the wrong time could lead one to be hospitalised. I believe he was having me on a bit; if I was to take him at his word, these fruits were as dangerous as the disposing of explosive devices. Obviously, he just didn't like prickly pears - and was successful in putting me right off them. I kept moving west, climbing some rolling hills before dropping down towards the peninsula of San Vito lo Capo. All rants about rubbish forgotten, I stopped, astonished at the incredible landscape where the stark shapes of Monte Cofano descended steeply towards idyllic coves, then disappearing into the sea. I was slower than usual, which means really slow. The transparency of the water was far too inviting and each day had to allow the time for a couple of good swims, with some cycling stuck in the middle in order to get somewhere. It did not take me too long to discover the works of art that emerged freshly baked from bakers' ovens. I stopped at one in the village of Custonaci and had a sort of introduction. There was nothing fancy about it; the shabby, wooden signpost at the entrance was humble and simply said 'traditional bread baked in wood burning ovens' but a steady stream of customers told me otherwise. The rustic vaulted interior was characterful, and inside a series of cabinets with sliding glass doors were all kinds of goodies on display.

Their names didn't mean much to me, so I asked the lady at the counter to pick what she fancied. I just asked for some to be salty and others sweet. The sweet ones were still warm, and the first bite was of a half moon fried pastry with a ricotta and chocolate filling that I later learnt was a 'Cassatina'. It lasted only three bites and was so good that I went right back to the counter and ordered another one. Everything else was as good and kept me cycling and cheerful for the rest of the day. I didn't break any long distance record, stopping in Lido Valderice. It was short of where I wanted to get to and the day was still early, but if I were to continue and follow my plans I would have had to cycle too much further. I felt hot and sweaty and the sight of more inviting beaches with more transparent water pulled me like a magnet and ground me to a halt. There was never a better time to be lazy.

- Erice, SICILY -

The original idea was to follow the flat coastline past the city of Trapani but, as I talked to a local cyclist, it was made clear that I couldn't possibly miss the town of Erice. Reading up a little more about it, it was clearly one of the most picturesque towns on the entire island. The historic town, set right on top of the only sizeable mountain, would take some effort to get to, but it sounded well worth it. I stopped at the crossroads and thought about it. The brain said forget it and keep to the nice beaches and the flat roads, while my guts told me off for being a wimp and that the right way was up the mountain. There was a third option, suggested by a local man who obviously didn't understand the commitment of a real cyclist.

"Go to Trapani and take the cable car to the top… You'll thank me for it!" he said.

Tempting words indeed, but I thought I should not give in to such comfort and started pedalling up a long straight road that took me to the foot of the climb. From there, a series of switchbacks made the gradients gentler and took me to the 750 metres altitude mark and to the jewel that is Erice. Drivers overtook me and encouraged me with short beeps on their horns, happy they were not the ones having to sweat whilst envious that I could stop where I wanted and take in the grand sea views, while they had to keep driving, missing most of it. After a couple of hours I finally passed the signpost that said 'Erice, city of peace and science'. I wandered along the narrow cobbled streets of the historic town, visiting its *duomo* as well as the well maintained castle. The effort had been certainly not wasted and there was more to come. The descent down the other side of the mountain was spectacular, with distant views of the Egadi islands and of the large city of Trapani down below. I sneaked through the city traffic as fast as I could, wanting to escape it quickly and get back to the sea. Nearby was the official start of Sibit, a cycle route that follows the southern coast all the way to Siracusa; and that months back had inspired me to come down here. I followed its first timid signposts that led me along country roads with less traffic.

A Dutch couple I met had expected it to be a dedicated cycleway and, used to different standards, were rather disappointed to have to share it with some traffic. Before Marsala it moved slightly off the coast, passing a series of impressive *saline*, shallow pools of sea water that evaporate, leaving grains of salt that are then heaped up into rounded piles.

      Navigating through villages using digital maps proved tricky in Sicily. Off the main streets there was usually an intricate maze of morphing roads and alleys that confused the best of satellites. At times it looked as if houses had been built first and then a road project had been rushed through later to connect them. For twenty minutes I followed a straight road that, according to my maps, should have reconnected with the main road a bit further on. All was well until I met a locked gate and, right in front of it, the entrance steps to a private property; an elegant villa had been conveniently built in the middle of my road without Google noticing it. Whether the road continued on the other side I would never know; I did a full turn and cycled twenty more minutes, back to where I had started.

      I arrived at Mazara del Vallo, a large town where I stopped to view the imposing Cathedral built by the Normans in a mixture of Romanesque, Baroque and Greek styles, something not unusual on an island with such a rich history. The town also boasted an elegant beach, with a narrow but long strip of sand that dived into a crystal clear sea. I displayed my solar panels and the New York licence plate for the first time - partly to charge my batteries but also to smile when hearing people's comments as I passed by.

"Look! New York! Did you see that!"

At that point there was usually a debate on how one could cross the Atlantic Ocean on a bicycle. Dressed as I was, it was easy to play the part of the foreigner and keep them wondering. Kids, after gathering round to spell each letter, looked at me with complete awe and admiration. As a kid growing up in a small provincial town myself, I really understood them; had I seen someone cycling past me with a New York plate at the time, I would have probably chased him out of excitement. Big cities, if possible somewhere very far away, were what I often dreamt about then.

In Selinunte I skipped another famous Greek temple and archeological site, opting for a relaxing swim and a lie down on a white sandy beach instead. I was not far from Agrigento and thought I should wait for its world renowned temples. Before that was the quaint village of Porto Palo, where the road snaked up to the top of the hill, playing with the shadows of the old watch tower. Out of season, the port had a melancholy beauty; just a sailboat could be seen far away, its white canvas puffed up by the wind, pushing it towards the horizon leaving back a vast blue emptiness. There was more swimming at a beach beyond Sciacca, and more delicious food to be tasted. Whether salty or sweet, it was often fried and involved a slower than normal digestion. I reached the large campsite at Eraclea Minoa where I met Massimo, who was cycling around Sicily with his girlfriend. Looking at my bike, he said he had seen a video of a guy riding something similar on the Carretera Austral in Patagonia. We figured out he was talking about me, which earned me an invitation to an evening barbecue, together with other campers they had just met the night before. It seemed the perfect place to stop and have a day off from the bike and just be lazy. I spent it as most Italians like to spend entire weeks in the summer, just laying flat on the sand, sunbathing. To ease the boredom, I took a long walk around the white cliffs to the silence of the secluded beach of Capo Bianco.

Once awake the following morning, I planned a quick goodbye to my barbecue hosts before setting off and making the most of the early hours cool temperature. Davide, Oriana and Lorenzo were the only ones awake. Davide put his extra large 'moka' on the camping stove, saying no Italian should start his day without a fresh coffee. One hour later we were still talking. I had revived his passion for cycling, something he told me he had done a little in his younger days. He was full of challenging plans:

"We should organise a trip to the Skeleton Highway!" he said, before going into a lengthy eulogy of the wild opportunities of the West African coast.

Lorenzo, on the other hand, was more interested in the Far East with all its 'herbs and spices'. As I mentioned past trips to the Indian Himalayas and to Pakistan, he said if I was to go again he would join me. Apparently the quality of smoke there was outstanding and, as he said, he always had spare time for travel and for getting high while cycling.

 A week of exposure had made me partially immune to the piles of rubbish and plastic bottles. Every now and then they appeared around the corner of a country lane, but one somehow got used to it. Maybe it was possible to turn a blind eye to it, in a place where I could swim on one of the best beaches I had ever seen and half an hour later be standing right in front of the imposing temple of Giunone in Agrigento. The beach was called 'La Scala dei Turchi', made famous by countless snapshots and television commercials that have turned it into a favourite tourist attraction. A little crowded for my taste, but on a mid-September day numbers were bearable. While the best section was reserved for those that could afford to come by boat, another side was accessible by walking down a footpath that started just off the main road. It gets its name from the dazzling white cliffs that wind and water have shaped into forms that resemble steps in a giant staircase that plunges into the pristine coral reef. After the swim it was a short bike ride to the outskirts of Agrigento, and its timeless ruins in the 'Valley of the Temples'.

 Just as a reminder that things are never quite perfect, the night spent at San Leone's campsite was far from peaceful. Right next to it was an open air disco where a live band was giving it all it had, playing a vast repertoire of Italian classics from the 60's and 70's that cut my sleep short and made me feel a little nostalgic. By the time they had run out of songs to play it was well past midnight. No wonder the early morning was abuzz with disgruntled Germans busy dismantling their carefully placed tents and canopies and determined to look for some peace elsewhere.

As I checked out I talked to the owner's son, who was also upset and eager to vent his frustrations about the state of the local bureaucracy. Apparently they kept pestering him with more taxes and new regulations.

"I wish dad was a Mafia boss instead." he told me.
"If he was, they wouldn't bother us as much…"

Beyond San Leone I moved inland, through extensive farms where at least plastic had been put to good use, turned into tunnels that speeded up the growth and ripening of fruit and vegetables. When the tunnels stopped, they were replaced by rows of solar panels and giant wind farms. Sadly I had just missed the fig season. There were a lot of fig trees about but they had been picked with the utmost care. All that was left were a few wrinkled fruits hanging on the furthest branches. Campsites so far had either been great or completely dishevelled, the latter usually rescued by good access to a spectacular beach. In the late afternoon I arrived and checked in to what looked like an example of the iffy type. Marco, another cyclist, joined me soon afterwards, pitching his tent nearby. Coming from opposite ends of the island, we shared information and tips on what we could look forward to as we progressed. In the morning the sun shined and I heard him call out:

"Come! Have a look at the field next to us."

A large mountain of rubbish and all kinds of waste had been piled up and set on fire by the same kind people who had welcomed us the previous night; columns of black smoke rose up, darkening the cloudless sky. Some German and Swedish guests who had spent the night in their caravans, were taking an early stroll and wondering why such a beautiful bonfire hadn't been scheduled for the previous night.

"How interesting." said a German lady with a smile.

She thought it must be just farmers burning grass or was wondering whether it was going to be barbecue day at the campsite. Instead, they were illegally disposing of rubbish, and it was a pretty sad sight to witness. Rubbish has always meant big business for the local mafia, and they seem to have taken 'control' of it. With no respect for nature, ignorant and short-sighted, they pollute their beautiful island and that very air they breathe. Recycling plants and incinerators built with public money are hardly opened before they become prime targets and get vandalised, leaving more piles of rubbish to be disposed of.

The route moved away from the coast again, surrounded by more greenhouses and thriving crops, enough to feed an entire country. I felt hot, and I only passed a single village in half a day - but luckily that village had a trickling fountain so that I could at least refill my bottle. It was much harder for some. Labourers were bent double to pick vegetables under the scorching sun, and I felt sorry for them and indignant over the lack of recognition for work that we take for granted. Next, the cycle route planners must have decided that passing by the ugly buildings of Gela's oil refinery, one of the largest in Italy, was a place worthy of sightseeing.

Back on the coast, *Luminoso* was the campsite that had been recommended by Marco. Spotlessly clean, he had told me. I must admit it was quite a step up from the 'bonfire' campsite, but while exceptional in services and facilities it was plagued by far too many insects. At breakfast, a couple from Verona offered me some freshly brewed coffee before my departure. We had a long chat whilst engaged in a balancing act of sipping the brew whilst at the same time clapping our hands to catch flies. Next to them was a caravan from Denmark. A man sat at the table on the veranda browsing a newspaper while committing insect genocide with a plastic fly-swot. Each strike was followed by a grin and he seemed to be having a great time.

I was now cycling in Inspector Montalbano's territory. The acclaimed television series had been a huge hit in Italy but had also found recognition internationally. Shot in Ragusa and in some of the most picturesque towns and villages around it, it had acted as a magnet for tourists, who set off on a sort of pilgrimage, in search of the original locations where filming had taken place. I seemed to be one of the few people to have never watched it. Still, the magnificence of Ibla Ragusa had existed long before Montalbano, and it will be there long after the inspector's feats have been completely forgotten.

- Ragusa, SICILY -

The old part of the town perched on the opposite hill appeared suddenly in front of me and I loved cycling and getting lost in its maze of cobbled streets. A few kilometres further on were two more wonders, the villages of Modica and Scicli. They were also part of the inspector's trail, with restaurants proud to advertise that our hero had dined here twice in series one and once in series three. Much more interesting, in Scicli's old cathedral they were about to celebrate a wedding; I sat down in the elegant square, admiring a crowd of proud friends, relatives, mothers and fathers dressed up in their best outfits; the bride kept everyone waiting and sweating past midday.

At Porto Palo di Capo Passero I realised I had reached the southernmost point of Italy. Some later research told me this was debatable if one considers some of the smaller Mediterranean islands: however, to reassure the doubtful, a stone with the official inscription forms the base of a Jesus Christ statue welcoming all with open arms. The plaque also claims that Ulysses docked here on his return from Troy; and, in what seems like an amazing coincidence, Saint Peter too reached it, on his way from Malta to Rome. This corner of the island also marks the division between the Mediterranean and the Ionian sea. I reached the Ionian after half a day of cycling through Pachino, a town renowned for some of the sweetest and most expensive tomatoes in the country. Cyclists I had met had recommended the campsite right by the beach, and it turned out to be a great find. Taking an early evening stroll along the beach I bumped into Lorenzo, whom I had met on the first day of my journey. I thought by now we must have gone our different ways, but there he was, sitting at a kiosk having a drink and writing his diary. He immediately recognised me and waved. I was curious to hear how it had all gone for him so far and whether he was still enjoying his first ever bike tour.

"It's been wonderful," he said, "I am having a blast."

This was remarkable, because the more he told me the more it was clear that he had experienced a fair amount of bad luck. A week before he had been chased by three aggressive dogs while cycling in the countryside. Another time, due to the dwindling light and some careless riding, he had hit a large rock and badly damaged his front wheel; this had forced him to walk for three hours to the town of Agrigento, the nearest place with a bike shop, where he had some hope of getting it fixed or replaced. Further on he broke his saddle and three spokes of the brand new wheel he had just purchased - and, as if this was not enough to put him off entirely, his left pedal cracked and was just about to fall off completely. His only regret was that he had spent more money on repairs than he had spent on the new bike, bought especially for the trip. Conscious that with these extra costs he had to save a little, he had pitched his tent on a beach on most nights. He shared with me a beautiful story of generosity. In Marsala, as evening was approaching, he stopped and asked an elderly man called Nino if there was a good place where he could pitch his tent. He told him to go a little further and look for a tower by the seaside, assuring him that it would be quiet and safe. He soon found it, and had hardly pitched his tent when a car parked nearby and started hooting repeatedly. He walked towards it and realised it was Nino.

"I thought about you, sleeping in a tent all night…" he told him.

"I am cooking some rabbit and potatoes tonight," he went on..

"They will be ready soon and I'll bring you some around eight thirty."

Punctually Nino returned, offering him a generous meal packed in a series of boxes together with a bottle of beer. He could hardly say thank you before Nino had left. In the morning there was more hooting.

"I thought of you and brought you some fresh pastries and a coffee."

"One cannot possibly cycle so far without breakfast."

I went back to my campsite while Lorenzo moved on, pushing his bike towards the beach, searching for a quiet patch of sand.

Although unaware of it, I seemed to have kept the best for last. Next day, hardly an hour away, I came to Marzamemi, a little port village whose central *piazza,* despite the restaurant tables, takes one back at least a couple of centuries. Antonio, the manager of a campsite I had stayed at a few days before, had recommended a couple of beaches not far away. I stopped at Vendicari, the first one, enjoying the sun and a swim in some of the most transparent waters seen thus far. To cool down a little, there was the unmissable ice cream van; the owner told me that no Sicilian tour would be complete without a visit to his hometown. Noto was a short detour from my original planned route and had to be earned by climbing a steep hill, but thankfully I listened to the advice and spent a couple of blissful hours wandering its elegant streets, and admiring its churches and palaces.

- *Noto, SICILY -*

The historic part of the town told a story of wealth and riches, clearly displayed in the highly decorated baroque palaces and San Nicolò cathedral. Each stone building was arranged to perfection, in matching tones of light sienna; nothing was out of place or jarring. From the top of the town centre it was all downhill back to the sea not far from the town of Avola and its renowned vineyards. Strangely, looking around me, I could only see olive trees. The final day of cycling was windy, with a night storm that shook my tent incessantly. I was kept awake by the bamboo groves, with leaves shaking and the weaker trunks snapping. By the morning the wind had gradually subsided but the sea was still rough and sombre. I cycled the peninsula of Punta del Gigante, facing the town of Siracusa. I first saw the city in the distance with the faint conic shape of Mount Etna that disappeared in the morning haze a little later. Eager for one last swim, I discovered the beautiful cove of Spiaggia del Minareto - just by chance, like most things on this bike trip. Siracusa began uninspiring, with anonymous blocks of flats and the heavy traffic typical of the suburbs in most Italian cities. Next, the bridge took me onto the island of Ortigia, the historic town centre, where everything changed and the ugly and the ordinary turned to the most sublime.

Northern Med

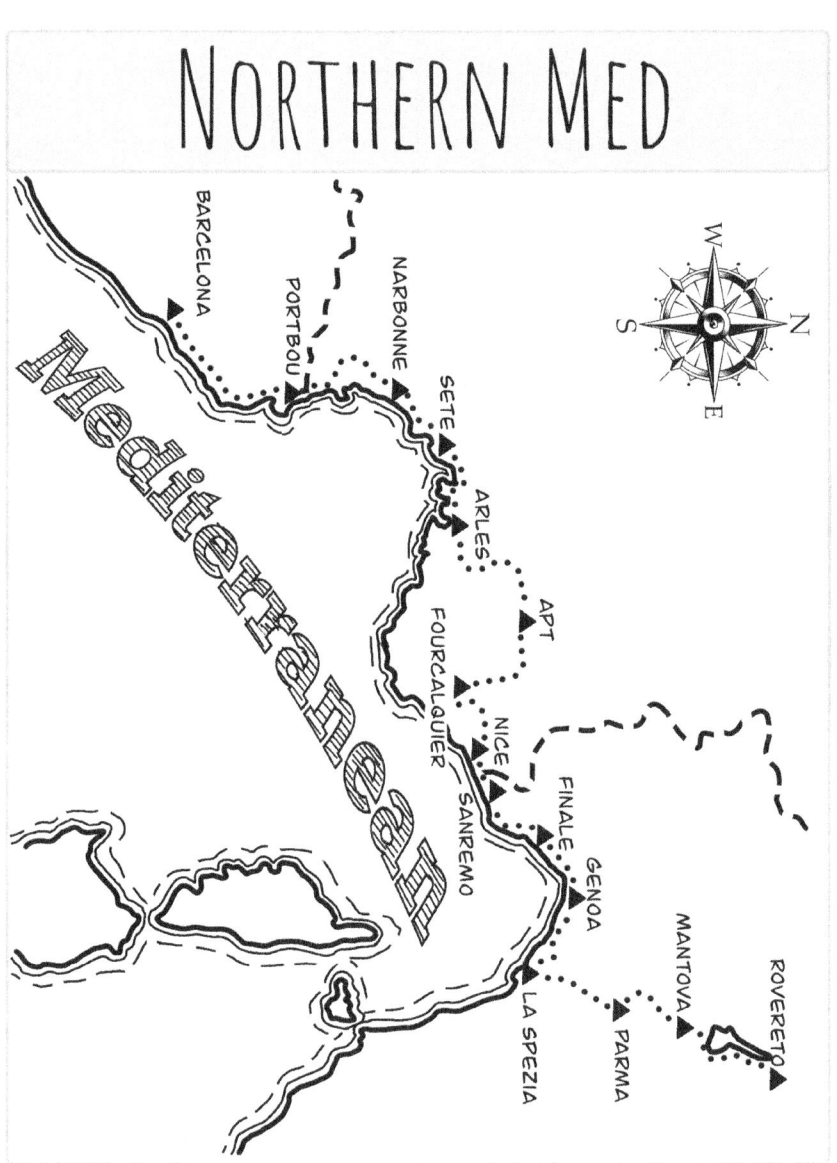

Northern Med

Barcelona deserved much more than a quick glance, but in the intense heat of summer I limited all sightseeing to a bare minimum of the Palau Nacional, Plaza d'Espanya and the unmissable glimpse of *la Sagrada Familia*. I expected a little more from this last site. Nothing to do with Gaudi's extravagant creativity and commitment. He had spent a lifetime working on it, dying when only a quarter was completed, and was buried in the crypt he had just built. What left me rather disappointed was the work of those who followed, thinking that it couldn't be left unfinished. Started in 1882, the project is still a work in progress and a series of tall cranes keep fiddling with it, adding new parts that stick out like a series of sore thumbs. However, days later I met someone who, on the contrary, had loved their visit. They suggested that next time I should give it a little more time; and that I should go inside, where the play of light and shadows brings those clumsy spaces to life.

Work had stopped again during an endless pandemic that had turned me into a sort of professional cyclist, sponsored through the generous handouts of the British government. With more time on my hands than I could handle I thought I would follow part of Eurovelo 8, also referred to as the Mediterranean Way. After the rewarding but chilly rides in southern England and the Scottish Highlands, I was pining for something a little warmer and a sea that I could safely dive into without risking frostbite. Starting in Gibraltar, Eurovelo 8 follows the coast all the way to Turkey, although I would have to take a shortened version and be satisfied to reach my hometown in northern Italy.

- Barcelona, SPAIN -

The coastal road out of Barcelona was flat and straight; it was a fast road, which allowed me to cover well over one hundred kilometres on the first day, even though I usually like to start a trip with a short ride. After Pineda del Mar I left the major road with its noisy traffic and turned right onto a smaller road, following the signposts pointing to *La Costa Brava*. At first it seemed just an ordinary coastline, but after Tossa de Mar the road started climbing above high cliffs with terrific views over idyllic bays.

From what I had heard, wild camping in Spain was illegal and had to be done with the utmost care. The common sense rules of putting up a tent late and dismantling it really early still applied, in order to avoid being caught. With no signs indicating any official campsite I took it gently: I had my first summer swim before climbing further up the mountains in search of a secluded patch of land. Looking at a map there was a picnic place on a narrow side road that looked promising. It turned out instead to be an archery practice ground with a covered shooting area and some decent wooden decking. I sat down to eat some food while trying to assess whether it was as quiet as it appeared to be. Large foam bullseye targets were haphazardly scattered all over the place as if the archers had to flee a gang of gun shooters. For a good couple of hours not a soul was seen or heard. Defying Spanish law once it got dark, up went the tent, pitched right in the middle of a messy shooting range.

I was woken up at 1 am by a distant conversation and a goodbye, followed by a door slammed shut and a car engine revving further up the mountain. Despite some experience, there are still times when a certain spookiness creeps in while camping alone in unfamiliar places in total darkness. Thoughts started racing; someone ill-intentioned must have been left behind and was now walking towards me. The inward chatter calmed down as the place regained its relative silence. An hour later I heard the sound of strumming chords on a badly tuned guitar playing a repetitive loop that wasn't going anywhere. It then fell quiet again until, in the early hours of the morning, I heard leaves crunching beneath heavy footsteps. It got louder and louder, as my imagination went into overdrive. If I had to die early, I thought I should at least face the culprit. I squeezed through the tent door and stood tall in a stalemate that seemed to last a lifetime. Unable to see anything around me, I heard more footsteps approaching; there was no doubt about it, they were coming from across the low fence that led into the forest. I stopped, and he or she stopped. My eyes, by now a little more used to the low light, finally discerned a faint white pattern that convinced me the serial killer had come to get me in a spotless white shirt. I uttered something stupid like "if you want to kill me get on with it and do it quickly…" when a loud snort and the head of a pony broke through the branches, just staring at me. I was so relieved my life had been spared! How on earth it could strum guitar chords, even if very badly, remained a complete mystery. The lesson learnt was to never camp alone without earplugs to block out unnecessary worries.

What remained of the Costa Brava was a string of nice beaches and quaint villages, andI stopped for a swim each time there was easy access with the bicycle. I decided to cross the border into France by following the coast; far more hilly than the option to move inland but certainly much more scenic. After Portbou, the final climb took me up the mountain pass that marked the border, now just a couple of abandoned cement buildings in the middle of the road, their walls covered in colourful graffiti. An army jeep was parked by the side of the road, and a couple of bored soldiers, relieved of their duties, nodded as I waved; and then I was in France, freewheeling down to the town of Cerbère. The hills rolled flatter and then disappeared into an endless stretch of sandy beaches. I reached Argelès sur Mer, where hoards of tourists crowded amusement parks and ferry wheels, bingeing on fried food and ice cream.

Two swimming stops meant I was a little late: having failed to find an open campsite, I decided the best option was to spend the night on the beach at Barcarès. I sat down on the still warm sand looking at another sunset. There were some frisbee players perfecting their throws, a couple of dog walkers and a few late swimmers, but they soon all vanished leaving the enormous stretch of sand deserted. It was time to erect the tent, and I opted for the threshold, beyond a wooden fence where the beach started. Sand proved most comfortable, fitting nicely around my back like the most expensive mattress. There was no need to cover the tent with the flysheet, giving me the chance to fall asleep while enjoying the spectacle of a starry night.

When deciding where to pitch the tent, my gut feeling had led me to resist the temptation to pitch it in the middle of the beach.

At what seemed an ungodly hour of the morning, I heard what sounded like a muffled helicopter.

I stood up and looked through the netting and couldn't believe my eyes; an extremely large vehicle with flashing lights of all shapes and colours was rolling towards me hardly one hundred metres away, as if from a scene of Close Encounters of the Third Kind. During the next hour of toing and froing around me, I realised that the high tech UFO was in fact an extra large sand plough. It had my unwavering attention. It projected rays of yellow light in circles and was topped by a few police-like blue sirens. At the front, there were a dozen headlights that scared me each time the machine turned and, beaming, moved again towards me. The monster was raking the sand tidy ready for the new day, pampering the beach so that it looked perfect. I was tense for a good hour while I was assessing each twist and turn, ready to abandon my shelter and leg it. After a final series of sweeping turns that blinded me and kept me worried, it did eventually move far enough away and I breathed a huge sigh of relief.

For the first time on the trip I left the Mediterranean and moved inland. The cycle route followed the footpath of a couple of canals, where traffic was pleasantly limited to boats and bicycles. First was the Canal de la Robine that ran through the pretty town of Narbonne; its most famous citizen was Charles Trenet, the singer who had made 'Douce France', a popular song I couldn't get out of my mind on a previous ride through France. I didn't want this trip to turn into a bad camping diary, and finally I was able to find a decent pitch at a campsite in Capestang. There were quite a few cyclists. I chatted with Thibaud, a Parisian chap who was doing his own Tour de France, making a proper loop around the country. It was quite impressive stuff, as he was proud to show me with the aid of his riding log, where he religiously noted departures, arrivals and mileage. The tally was approaching three thousand kilometres, a bit over halfway on his itinerary back to Paris.

In the heat of summer, the solar panels and New York registration plate were back on display.

"*T'as vu?! New York!*" "Did you see?! New York!"

As usual, when adults asked, I would tell the truth and say it served as a weight to keep my panels from flapping and closing. I reserved my lies for children, as I thought they could do with a little dreaming and I did not want to disappoint them. From Capestang it was time to join the Canal du Midi that would eventually get me back to the sea. Considered one of the greatest engineering feats of the 17th century, it starts at the Atlantic Ocean and allows boats to cut through to the Mediterranean without having to travel all the way south around Spain. Upsetting as it must have been to the Spanish, the shortcut was a busy place full of happy sailors and people on vacation that could save weeks of their holidays.

     I cut across a corner of La Camargue with its wild white horses and pink flamingos. I was wary of the stagnant waters and marshes as they are the perfect breeding ground for mosquitoes, especially in the heat of summer. They made the most of my calves when I stopped but, like their Scottish siblings, they couldn't keep up once I was cycling. The cycle route followed long, thin strips of land that were like natural bridges, with water on either side, before reaching the Canal du Rhone. I felt hot. Under a scorching midday sun, and with no shade, I had almost run out of water when four boaters sitting on the path offered me some chilled white wine; they reassured me that there was a running fountain within a short distance. I had planned to spend the night at Saint Giles campsite.. As I registered, the friendly owner warned me that Saturday night meant live music until midnight. I nodded halfheartedly, selfishly hoping the weather forecasts that were predicting a particularly stormy night were right. Whilst I set up my tent, dark clouds gathered, clearly moving our way. Rain pelted down punctually at nine o'clock, bringing to a halt the first thumping beats that had started blasting from a beefy sound system. Nothing could be done about the other nuisance. The campsite was well aligned with Nimes airport's runway and jet engines roared more than usual as pilots struggled to cope with the side winds and land on such a bad night. It was just a short ride from Saint Giles to Arles, a day that allowed me to follow some of the landmarks associated with Van Gogh, my favourite artist. He had lived in Arles for fifteen months and there he created some of his most well known paintings. He had deliberately chosen southern France, struck by the vivid light and hues of the landscape, and I shared these feelings while cycling. It is all about the sun and the blue skies, and a light that can turn even barren soil or tall grass into something beautiful and interesting. Arles is in itself an interesting city, rich in history, dating back to Roman times when it was one of the main centres of Gaul.

- Arles, FRANCE -

An ancient and well preserved Roman Arena stands right in the centre, surrounded by the large historic core of the town, built on one side of the river Rhone. I cycled further into the region of Provence and reached Saint Remy, one of its main touristic hubs. Nearby is the Saint Paul monastery and the mental institution where Van Gogh self-admitted and sojourned for a year after suffering a major breakdown. I had already visited it years before so I kept cycling towards the undulating blue shapes of the Alpilles mountains, through fields of wheat and sunflowers that seemed like a re-creation of many of his paintings. I crossed groves of pine forest and thought that surely, he also must have heard the same deafening yet relaxing noise of the crickets.

I passed through picture-perfect landscapes with ancient churches, orchards and vineyards, and the quintessential fields of mauve lavender colouring the Provençal landscape. Forcalquier's campsite turned out to be full even for a lone cyclist. I had as good a meal as I could manage and resigned myself to finding a hidden place to spend the night in my tent. In the end there was no need for stealth camping. A friendly farmer was mowing the lawn by his front gate; we started chatting and I decided to ask if I could use a bit of his land. The quick chat was hopefully enough for him to decide that I wasn't going to be a nuisance and he pointed out a couple of fields, telling me I could pick the one I most liked. He showed me where I could find some water and pointed to a table and chairs, saying I was welcome to use them if I wanted to. I thanked him and said goodbye, promising to disappear without a trace by seven thirty in the morning. I maintained my promise to leave early and carried on following the small roads of the Luberon mountains, popular with hikers, climbers and cyclists. On top of a peak in the distance, the metallic silver sphere of Saint Michel Observatory was sparkling in the sunlight, strategically placed where lights wouldn't pollute the night sky. Rumours of a forthcoming storm made me stop cycling early at La Verdière. It was just a tiny village in the *Parc National du Verdon* with a glorious old bakery and an elegant campsite with a swimming pool that seemed the perfect place to take a break.

A cycling family arrived soon after me, mom and dad pulling heavy trailers with all the luggage while their ten year old daughter cycled between them on her own little bike. I spoke to them and realised they had done several tours before, but somehow this time things hadn't gone according to plan and they got lost along the way. They had set off from Draguignan few days earlier, but dad's phone, with the carefully planned route and the digital maps, had slipped from his hands while taking a picture from a tall bridge on the first day. From then on they had been going from signpost to signpost, trying to follow the Mediterranean Way as best they could, and often failing. As predicted, it did rain most of the following day and, despite feeling a little restless stuck inside the tent, I thanked Resources and Planning for the timely decision to stay put, happy that I hadn't been caught in the rain while cycling.

Once the weather had cleared up, I was back on Brutus, heading towards the Côte d'Azur and almost sniffing Italy. Draguignan didn't seem a particularly attractive place, but it was remarkably green for a large city. Thick pine forests climbed the gentle slopes all around the city, bathing the landscape in fluorescent greens. I knew that from then on the cycleway would start climbing. At a certain point I missed a turn and, after I had backtracked but failed to find it, I asked an elderly man. He pointed to a cement track that was rising straight and steep a little further on.

"That can't possibly be a cycle route. " I said firmly in my best French.

He said it was indeed, but also encouraged me by saying that calvary was just a kilometre long and would then join a decent road. There are times when I wonder what motivates the people in charge of planning these cycle routes: maybe the incompetence of having never ridden a bicycle or the delight in causing pure frustration and pain? Whatever the answer, I had to get off the bike and bent double over it, start to push my load uphill, like a miner pushing a cart up a steep mineshaft.

After a lengthy meander up the hills and through the quaint villages of *Var* and *Alpes Maritimes*, I reached the top of a mountain ridge, and from there started my descent on a rough and steep trail. Halfway down, I encountered a barrier blocking the way with a warning sign saying that it was too dangerous to continue due to the high risk of fire. Were the cycle-route planners, who had failed to defeat me with ridiculous grades, now attempting to set me on fire?
Looking at the map, the only alternative was to retrace my steps, which would have involved a long slog back up the mountain to the ridge where the descent had started. In the heat of the midday sun, I weighed up my options. Risk of dehydration and a possible heart attack, or risk to cycle through thick smoke and flames. Crucially, only one option was downhill so I decided to push on, ignoring health and safety. I sped down to Mandelieu la Napoule, where the Mediterranean Way took me safely back to the sea.

Following the peace and quiet of the previous few days, Cannes at the height of summer felt like carnage, with bodies and towels filling every available inch on a thin strip of sand. I was reminded of the annual summer holidays spent with my parents, basted in greasy sun lotion, sizzling under the sun for the sake of a perfect tan. It felt like a lifetime. I still loved the sun, together with a good swim and a place to stretch out on the beach but it had to be done in moderation. I was definitely the odd one out here; most seemed to be relishing it, using their hard-earned savings to afford the extravagant *Côte d'Azur* prices. I stopped for a swim at posh Cap d'Antibes before starting a vain search for a bargain stay in the midst of utter luxury. I knew it was going to be a challenge. It got later and later as I kept cycling along the beautiful coastline, until the sun began to set. Along a quieter section of the road, some people were setting up their folding chairs and tables on the pavement by their parked camper-vans. I stopped for a chat, and it was clear that I had arrived just at the right time, when cocktails were about to be served followed by dinner. They were part of an ever growing trend of people who had given up expensive lifestyles and mortgages to live in vehicles, usually parked in the most stunning of places. There were Luana and Max, a young French couple, and an elderly man called Luc who had spent the last fifteen years in his white Ford Transit van. They had already stationed themselves there for a few nights, and told me that it was quiet enough at night. Having failed to secure my luxurious villa stay for the night, I thanked them for sharing a bit of their lives with me and some delicious *mojitos* and crossed over the road barrier, setting up my tent on a flat slate of rock by the seaside.

At 5am I had my earliest dip ever, swimming before sunrise off Cagnes sur Mer. I used the convenient beach showers to wash away the previous day's grime and, after breakfast at a café and the mandatory launderette stop in Nice, I moved on towards ever more glamorous places. Saint Jean Cap Ferrat was followed by Cap d'Ail and then a border crossing into the *Principauté de Monaco*. The cycleway route steered away from Montecarlo but, for the sake of adding one more country to my list, and out of a perverse curiosity, I thought I would cycle right through it. I used to enjoy watching Formula One car racing, and I felt spurts of adrenaline as I sped through the circuit at incredibly low speeds. The place, elegant as it was, seemed a bit of a building site. Roadworks were ongoing and long tunnels were being excavated to cope with the increasing traffic, while space for tall and thin new buildings was found by gnawing away at the mountain. Despite the place's racing pedigree, there was a constant gridlock of traffic, full of frustrated drivers who, despite their Porsches and Ferraris, couldn't really get anywhere.

Much better, if one could afford it, was to turn up aboard a large yacht at the Marina instead; preferably thirty metres long to avoid any inferiority complex. Montecarlo was exactly as I'd expected; a place of blond, tanned people whose greatest fun was to stroll along the main street comparing their designer clothes, handbags, sunglasses, necklaces and jewel studded watches. Every now and then the noise and buzz was shaken by the mighty rumble of an engine. - more Ferrari or Porsche drivers, powerless and stuck in traffic like everybody else despite their powerful engines and all the money they had spent. It was a joy to ride past traffic jam after traffic jam, in a permanent overtaking manoeuvre that meant Brutus and I were clearly the fastest on the day in Montecarlo. Everything in the place was expensive, and had to be paid in an obscure currency, perhaps gold or diamonds? Happy to have seen it, I made sure to escape fast, without touching anything in order to avoid any charges. I was soon back in France, but not for long; half an hour later I crossed the border into Italy, proud of having crossed three countries between morning and lunchtime.

I regretted having to leave France, as I was rekindling my passion for and fluency in the language. However, crossing countries was otherwise seamless and hardly noticed; it was still the same sea but now populated with Italians, which meant a bit more chaos and cars double parking. The route between Ventimiglia and Sanremo started out as nice as I had imagined; a wonderful cycleway carved along the edge of the coastline, followed by an incredible series of long, lit tunnels. These offered a good respite from the noise and traffic and were the perfect places to keep cool in the midst of summer. The last tunnel, maybe the longest, took me a while to cycle through: the minuscule bright dot at the end of it grew larger and larger until it exploded in the full brightness of Sanremo, renowned in Italy as the city of flowers. Because of its reputation, it had to work hard keeping up the highest standards; floral displays in full bloom lent their fantastic colours to the seaside. Beyond Sanremo, the official route of the Mediterranean Way veered inland towards Piemonte and its mountains. Cycling Liguria's coast, a narrow strip of land squeezed between the mountains and the sea, takes a bit of courage and is not for the faint-hearted. In limited space shared with a large motorway and the railway, what is left for cyclists is the glorious *Via Aurelia*, National Road 1, a title well earned thanks to having been one of the main Roman roads, connecting the Eternal City to Gaul. Two thousand years later, I bet ancient Romans would have felt utterly disappointed to know that in summer, their heroic construction effort is just gridlocked, often used as a parking lot to reach the best beaches and coves. The seaside really looked gorgeous, and during the worst of the traffic I often stopped and jumped into the water. The best spots were usually the most inaccessible, like Cervo and Noli; they had to be earned with a jolly good scramble down a steep mountain, hanging precariously onto rocks and thorny bushes. They were not really accessible on a bicycle, but at my slow speed I was usually able to spot somewhere scenic that was not life threatening. Another instance where owning a large yacht might have come in handy.

About halfway along Liguria I reached the regional capital of Genoa. Like anywhere else here, it had had to adapt to the morphology of the terrain, expanding into a long thin strip of a city between the rocks and the sea. Crossing it from one end to the other took me most of the morning. I noticed how the long days of summer cycling were taking a toll on my forearms that by now had turned purple and looked like two boiled lobsters. To give them a break from another scorcher, I sought shelter in the botanic gardens of Nervi, indulging in one of my favourite summer inactivities: lying on shady park benches while listening to the crickets chirping. After the town of Rapallo, another glamorous section of the coast started in Santa Margherita. Next to it is tiny and exclusive Portofino, a quaint little port but also a great testament to the wonders of marketing. I reached it as mortals do, from the twisting road that leaves Santa Margherita. The proper way to access it would of course have been to moor a large boat at a fair distance and then to call a taxi boat to drop you off by the terrace of your favourite restaurant. What was once just a cute fishing port is nowadays one of the best places to show off VIP status and stardom; given the bounty of cash around, I would also assume it is one of the best places in the world to be a restaurant waiter. It was a *bonsai* Montecarlo where folks in Armani suits and Rolex watches strolled proudly around the little square, just to be noticed. I put on my best stroll, pushing a tiny bike that seemed completely out of place. In the end it was well worth it. Bjorn Borg, an old tennis hero of mine, was standing thoughtful in front of a restaurant's menu, looking dismayed by such expensive courses. Staying close to the coast meant I hadn't really climbed many hills. This changed once in Sestri, where I noticed the road getting steeper and steeper on its way to Passo Bracco at an altitude of 700 metres. This was not usually something I would worry about, but with the heat and some nasty gradients it proved challenging. I didn't help myself by taking a wrong turn at a diversion, starting a reckless descent that ended up going nowhere. It took me some time to realise my mistake and to come to terms with the fact that there was no alternative route I could follow, and I had to slog all the way back up, hoping I wouldn't melt in a puddle of sweat. It could have been worse. Two young French girls I met at the campsite had taken a different wrong turn and ended up risking their lives, following a series of long tunnels on a major road that was banned to cyclists.

"We did see the warning signs…" they told me.

Still, they pressed on until just past the second tunnel, when a man in a pickup van offered them a lift to safety, telling them they were too young to die. Back on my own journey, I eventually took the right descent down the coast, reaching the village of Framura where an elevator takes you up to yet another disused railway track with tunnels, which offered a much more peaceful ride for cyclists and pedestrians. I was also told that along this part were some of the best beaches Liguria had to offer. There were stunning coves at Bonassola and at Levanto, so I thought I would stop for a couple of days to make the most of it, before going up and down the mountains of Cinque Terre, finally descending into the town of La Spezia and to the border of Liguria.

- Manarola, ITALY -

The Cinque Terre route was worth the extra effort, with great views over the world famous five villages perched over the sea. A closer visit entailed a steep walk down the mountain followed by a gruelling scramble back up to continue cycling. I picked Manarola as it was the easiest one to reach and a bit less popular, which in August meant smaller crowds of tourists. There are times when a bicycle is a hindrance. Each village is much more accessible by train, along a track that clings to the cliffs and, as an engineering feat, is a close match for those incredible trains I had seen climbing the Swiss Alps. I left Manarola with the strong wish to have another chance to visit the Cinque Terre, on foot and outside peak season.

The descent to the large town of La Spezia was fast, and at times opened excellent views over the bay and its port, which is one of the busiest in Italy and a convenient stop for cruise liners. A milestone by the side of the road said that it was 450 kilometres to Rome, but I was not going that way and it was time to leave the Aurelia and part with the Mediterranean. Next I had to cross the Apennine mountains and head North towards Lake Garda before eventually reaching home.

The entrance gate to the campsite near Pontremoli, at the foot of La Cisa pass, was locked shut due to the pandemic, with a notice saying that they would be waiting for me next summer. As I stood by a quaint old church with a cemetery, gauging my options for the night, I saw a signpost and realised I was at one of the main stages of the Via Francigena, a pilgrimage route that starts in Canterbury and cuts through the middle of Europe on its way to Rome. With dwindling light, I spotted a priest walking out of the church gate and asked if he could spare a corner of his lawn. Most friendly and accommodating, and maybe assuming I must be a pilgrim on a bicycle, he said it was not a problem and that he would look forward to seeing me at Mass the following morning at seven. I nodded, a little vaguely.

A new day started and I made sure to leave by six, not only to avoid morning service but also because a long mountain climb lay ahead. Despite being well trained and fit, the thousand metre climb was better done in leisurely fashion and in cooler temperatures. Beyond, there was an enjoyable descent to the great plains of the Pianura Padana and a stop to visit the attractive historic centre of Parma. A little further North I rejoined the Eurovelo 8 route that I had left in France. Here, it was a trail that followed the course of the Po river, the largest river in the country. Despite being determined to get a proper room for the night, and a badly needed wash, things didn't work out. I met a local cyclist who convinced me that a little further on there was a perfect and peaceful place to stay.

"Keep going until you see a tall monument," he said, "then take the side road that goes right down to the river and you will find a wooden cabin and a few fishermen's boats."

"There won't be anyone there on a Monday and there's also a well with water if you ever need to wash…" he said discerningly.

I reached it at dusk. A few cars were in fact parked along the road, with a group of youngsters drinking beer and enjoying the evening breeze. Too tired to go any further, I sat down and started chatting with them; they were most friendly and confirmed it was a good place and that it was unlikely anybody would turn up at night… As it got darker all cars and people vanished and I was left alone with the river and its majestic flow through the plains. However, the peace and serenity didn't continue through the night. After midnight a trickle of cars arrived and parked not too far away, often flooding my tent with their headlights. The last one turned out to be the most spooky. Thinking I was having a nightmare, I heard yet another engine revving and another car approaching; I looked at my watch and it was 3am. Someone slammed the door shut and belted out an angry shout into the silent night; I tried to calm my jitters, thinking that surely I didn't deserve to die just a few days away from home. A heated phone conversation followed with lots of toing and froing, then luckily the individual somehow calmed down. I was still left in a ten minutes limbo of silence that seemed to last a lifetime. Eventually, with great relief, I heard another door slam, then an engine starting up, and I knew I had survived.

I stopped in Mantua to visit a colleague and joined her friends and family for a meal that almost brought tears to my eyes after weeks of cold meals and assorted sandwiches. The final stretch along the Mincio river, near the southern tip of Lake Garda, brought back familiar memories of the territory, its people and their accent. With temperatures in the low forties, these were the two hottest days of that

Italian summer. I reached Peschiera just in time for the last sunset and a final night at a campsite. For the last day, what a better welcome back than the scenic road bordering the eastern side of the lake, a road I used to ride frantically fast along on a light racing bike, in what now seemed like another lifetime. Now, no longer trying to break any personal records, there was no reason to hurry, just the joyful knowledge that I would soon arrive.

* * *

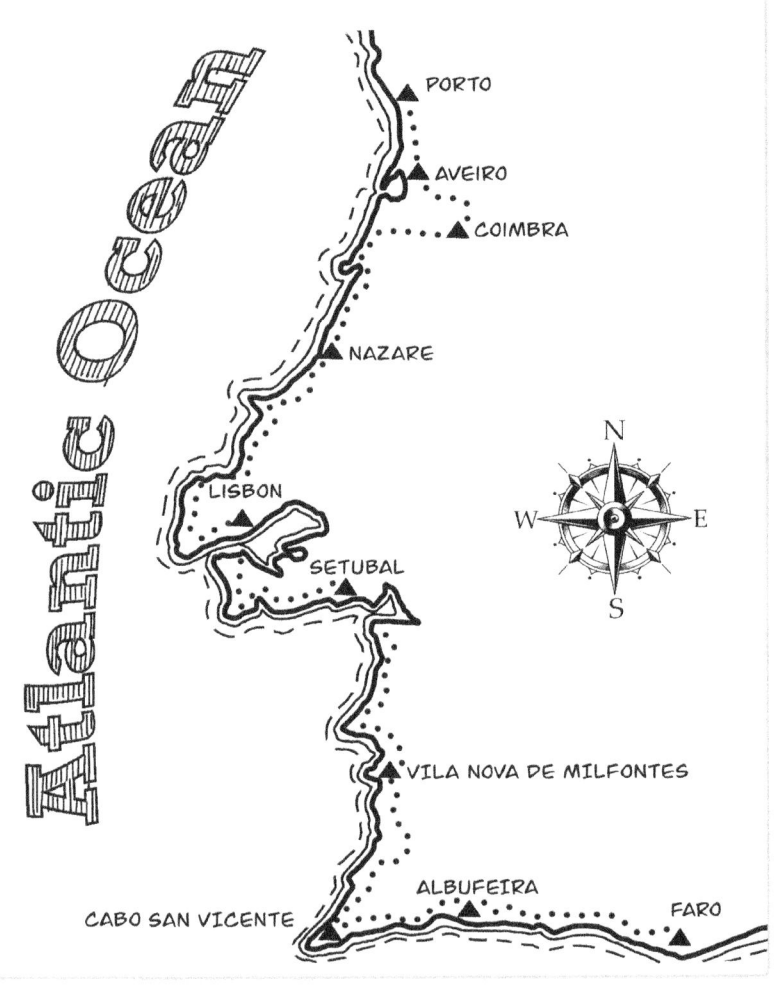

Portugal's Coast

Taking a break after the first morning of cycling, I am listening to the roaring waves crashing onto the shores of Albufeira. I had been reading how the Algarve, the southernmost region of Portugal, gets more sunny days per year than California and, since it's within easy reach for me, I thought it would provide some respite from winter. Off season, there were no colourful towels and bodies sunbathing on the sandy beach but, given it was the end of January, temperatures were balmy and a far cry from the damp cold I had left behind. I had reached Faro the previous day in the late afternoon and, given the short winter days, decided to stay not far from the airport. I checked in late at a Youth hostel that turned out to be a sunny hideaway for septuagenarians. The kitchen was buzzing with pensioners who had plenty of time on their hands, a steady income from their pensions and, despite the recent plague, were looking remarkably healthy. Juergen, a retired teacher from Hamburg, was relaxing in the sitting area. He had left home four months earlier, cycled down along the Atlantic coast, and was now sitting out winter in Faro before heading back north along the Mediterranean coast. My roommate was Eric, a Frenchman who similarly had escaped the chills of Bayonne's winter and was biding his time in southern Portugal, waiting for spring before making a string of train journeys to return home.

I was adding to my recent collection of Eurovelo cycle routes. This was Eurovelo number 1, following the length of the Atlantic coast from the north of France to the bottom tip of Portugal. I should have thought that, as a first effort, the European authorities would have paid extra attention to ensure that no one got lost trying to follow it but I was going to be proved wrong. Hardly had I left Faro when a signpost pointed me towards a pine forest and left me stranded in a maze of sandy trails leading nowhere. What should have been hardly ten kilometres turned into twenty and thirty as I backtracked to regain my bearings. Eventually I re-emerged in sanitised Quinta do Lago, a tidy place where I seemed to be the only one not into golfing. Accurately forecast, a nine knots easterly wind helped me gather speed, and pushed me further than I had planned, reaching the quaint town of Lagos just as daylight was fading. On the Sunday morning, I woke up when most people were going to bed after partying on a night out. I wandered around the empty streets of Lagos, where even cobblestones are turned into a work of art, arranged in shiny and elegant mosaic patterns. Leaving town I gave up trying to faithfully follow the cycle route as it took far too much patience. Once I had missed the track the first time, I just kept going, and I made much better progress than if I had fiddled with the maps and put up with all the required back and forths.

I reached Sagres just in time for lunch. I ate outside a restaurant's sitting area, basking in the warmth of the winter sun. It looked like a perfect, chilled surfing town, where even a late January day didn't bring any hint of sadness. In Sagres, tall waves and plenty of sunshine is all that's needed, together of course with the ability to find balance while standing on a surfboard. In the afternoon I went a little further along the peninsula, reaching Fortaleza and Cabo San Vincente, with its charming lighthouse set on the southernmost point of mainland Portugal. A dirt track whisked me back in a loop to where I had started and, from then on, it rejoined the coastline, this time heading North, towards Lisbon and eventually Porto. I had almost forgotten all about the Eurovelo route when finally, on the third day of cycling, I spotted a sign with clear white lettering over a blue European flag. Hardly one hundred metres further on I found another one and then another, as if somebody had felt sorry and wanted to make amends for the sloppy work back in the Algarve.

- Cabo San Vicente, PORTUGAL -

A glance at the map showed me that the road near Carrapateira would eventually wind through a nature reserve along coves and beaches; I knew it was time to use the tent I carried and relished a break from strangers snoring and all the door slamming that are part and parcel of nights in a hostel. At night I had a series of odd dreams, perhaps triggered by the sound of the waves or of the tent flapping. The most memorable involved something I am familiar with, the Tokyo transport system. It was nothing like the real thing mind you! Japan is a haven of health and safety and pushes ease and comfort to extremes, yet in my dream, train and subway journeys involved stations whose platforms had to be accessed with life threatening acrobatics. Getting off a train was the beginning of a perilous journey.

There were no lifts to access the different floors; platforms had to be reached by clinging to slippery plumbing pipes or balancing on precarious metal frames and wobbly scaffolding. I was scared to death by the heights involved in trying to make a train connection, while a crowd of Japanese salarymen were happily climbing up and down like spiders, clad in immaculately ironed office suits and white shirts while holding their office leather briefcase. I wasn't particularly keen to know what it all meant, if anything. Maybe a remnant of a pandemic that clearly showed that life is precarious. I was aroused by footsteps trampling down the wooden walkway next to where I had pitched my tent, followed by the flash of a torch lighting up the darkness. The culprit turned out to be just a fisherman while I was relieved to find myself lying flat and well grounded on the soil of a Portuguese beach. I packed up my tent just as more fishermen were filling up their buckets with their catch and started to ride along Rota Vicentina, which followed the contour of the coastline, with steep descents and sudden climbs that reminded me of recent gruelling rides in Cornwall.

The Eurovelo route was now meticulously marked with metal signposts so frequent that it seemed as if those in charge had suddenly found some lost stock which needed to be put to immediate use. Most were unnecessary, in places when even trying to get lost would have been impossible. Surely half of them should have been sent down to Faro where they were badly needed and could have been put to better use. At a point along a country lane a sign pointed right up a steep hill in what seemed like a good prank pulled by some particularly naughty children. I pushed the bike up the silly gradient, cycled on a little just to realise that I was lost again, pushing my bike through mile long rows of dark purple Lollo Rosso lettuce. The soil got softer and softer until I found myself walking on sand dunes, cursing loudly at the relevant European Institutions. Emerging from the fields, I once more gave in to the ease of a main road, lined by rows of tall eucalyptus trees whose scent made me recall past sunny days in California. I called it a day in Zambujeira do Mar and checked into a hostel where I was the only cyclist amongst a handful of long distance hikers. All had left

Lisbon and were heading south, having a great time despite foot blisters and complaints of sinking sands. I knew what they were talking about.

I had breakfast with the hikers while discussing the pros and cons of hiking versus cycling; they gasped at my plan to reach Sines by the end of the day when it had taken them lots of sweat and four days to cover the distance. On the other hand, I told them that at times I wished I could stick to the coastline as much as they could and not have to take misleading diversions through fields of lettuce. I felt sorry for their foot blisters and they felt sorry for my aching bottom. By the time breakfast was over we had called it a tie and at least agreed that life is never quite perfect. I left and was soon wandering past the colourful buildings and through the winding streets of the beautiful village of Vila Nova de Milfontes. Otherwise the rest of the day would have been unremarkable but for the best seaside views so far in Porto Covo and a delicious *'plato do dia'*, from the menu of the day at a roadside restaurant. Not really understanding the menu has the advantage of providing plenty of surprises once the meal is served. Near the town of Sines, with its energy plants and large commercial port, the scenery verged on the ugly and, while navigating a large roundabout, I heard the ominous sound of the first flat tire. That is another advantage I gave to the hikers; they might get blisters but don't get punctures! I sat down on a concrete bollard between the busy road and an industrial complex and fixed the hole under the sunshine.

Sines' claim to fame was that in the 15th century it gave birth to the great explorer Vasco da Gama, but it seems fair to say that it has lost its shine since. It wasn't quite the picturesque seaside town I had expected so I pushed past it, in search of an elusive hotel room. Soon after the winter sunset the light quickly vanished, and I was left with a familiar back up plan, hiding my tent somewhere under the pine trees. The following day I was up and packed early, and started riding on roads that had been planned by drawing straight lines on a map with a ruler. Tatiana, one of the hikers, had mentioned the endless straight trails that ran parallel, so long that she had to entertain herself with a series of podcasts. It was boring enough when cycling, and I am sure it must have been hellish at five kilometres an hour. I reached Troia, such a terrible word for an Italian that it is hard to say it out loud, just in time to take my first ferry to bridge a thin strip of sea and reach the town of Setubal. I could have pushed further on, but Lisbon was now only a day away so I decided to not rush it. First impressions were misleading. The town seemed dwarfed by ugly structures and by the large port a little further along the coastline; however, a short stroll around the city centre made me realise that my first impressions were wrong and that it was a place worth discovering.

Getting into Lisbon seemed straightforward; a quiet start along a small road following the coast, then a bit of a battle with the traffic of the suburbs before a ferry trip across a thin strip of Atlantic Ocean into Lisbon harbour. The start out of Setubal was as good as I had hoped for. Scenically it was one of the best roads so far, and although it was early morning I wondered why it had hardly any traffic. After ten kilometres the reason became clear; one hundred metres before a tunnel, a metal fence with thick chains and bolts interrupted my joyful ride. I didn't fancy going back all the way and the alternative route involved leaving the coast. A bike can usually get through places where cars can't, I thought. I managed to shift one side of the barrier a little and squeezed through the small opening. As it turned out it was a wasted effort because once I reached the tunnel I was met by a second set of barriers. Unlike the first one these were bolted properly to the ground leaving me no chance of getting through. I tried to see if I could walk around the tunnel by riding down to the beach and pushing the bike along a thin strip of sand between the rocks and the sea. I pushed the bike slowly, with tires sinking, until the sand ran out and I was again stuck, this time blocked by vertical rocks plunging into the sea. I walked back sulking and feeling let down by my stubborn streak. I climbed back up to the road in a foul mood just as a lady, whom I thought must be part of the conspiracy to not let me continue as I pleased, was opening the gate to park her car; she must have also had a challenging morning as she started shouting in Portuguese, most likely telling me I shouldn't have been where I was. A perfectly fair point, but not something taken lightly by a stuck cyclist whose socks were by then full of sand. I shouted back in some stroppy English, saying that I wouldn't be where I was had I seen any road sign earlier, telling me the road was closed. Admittedly with my limited Portuguese there might well have been one somewhere and it wasn't really her fault. Going back was the only way after all; changing route, I headed to Lisbon the ugly way, fast and straight, mostly on emergency lanes full of debris. Once I reached Cacilhas, a ferry crossing took me across to the capital's centre, and I looked forward to a day off exploring the city.

- Lisbon, PORTUGAL -

The historic part of Lisbon was not built for cyclists, or ladies in high heels for that matter. The central quarters of Castelo and Alfama, where I was staying, are built on a series of steep hills with plenty of steps, walkways and lanes paved with some of the most treacherous and uneven cobblestones I had ever seen. A couple of hidden lifts, if you ever find them, let you gain some height, but otherwise you have to negotiate the wonky steps and streets at your own peril. But it was a price worth paying to experience this city, with its long history. There was a lot of huffing and puffing from people struggling up and down the steep hills while carrying their shopping; every now and then someone stumbled, producing what I am sure was some colourful Portuguese. Bicycles are usually a fast way to explore, but riding my folding bike here verged on the pathetic. Besides the constant shaking, the bike's folding system was clearly not enjoying Lisbon as much as I was. My arrival was announced by a mighty rattle, attracting far too much attention. Equally treacherous were the tram rails crisscrossing the main streets: I had to pay careful attention not to let the front wheel slip into one of them, leading to an embarrassing fall and a fast visit to Accident and Emergency. Health and safety seemed to take priority even for the most elegant of women, wearing practical flat soled shoes or even sneakers.

Back at the hostel I spent a couple of hours chatting to Laurent, a Frenchman from Brittany. We shared a passion for adventure travel and had both been to some unusual destinations. He told me he had been inspired by the Swiss writer Nicolas Bouvier and his travel accounts in a book titled 'The Way of the World'. When he was in his late forties, he decided to undertake a similar trip, driving a 4x4 car from France all the way to Cambodia. Some of his favourite memories during that trip were located in those little villages in Gilgit Baltistan in Pakistan, villages that I had also come to know on my bike. He had also driven up Babusar pass a few decades earlier than I had, at a time when the road was a little more than a single track and still unsurfaced.

As a Frenchman, Laurent was understandably extremely annoyed at how the world had accepted the English language as lingua franca.

"It's distorting people's cultures," he told me.

I suggested it was quite handy to be able to communicate no matter where one was in the world, but I was just rubbing salt into an injury and he started arguing with history.

"It all started when we sold Louisiana to the United States," he said, bitterly.
"If we hadn't, the world would be a very different place..."
"Well...maybe it is just being French..." he admitted.
"It would be so much easier if everyone spoke French instead."

Leaving Lisbon, heading north, was a much more pleasant affair than arriving. I had already tested the nice coastal cycleway to Belem while sightseeing; I followed it, passing under the *Ponte 25 de Abril*, the bridge that crosses the strait and leads to the imposing statue of *Cristo Rei* set on top of a hill and welcoming everyone with its open arms. Eventually I joined a larger road with some traffic but also lots of cyclists enjoying a Saturday morning ride. Cascais was the last buzzing seaside resort town and after that I was back to a quiet cycleway heading towards Nossa Senhora do Cabo, where I took a diversion into the mountains of Cascais Nature Park in order to visit the historic town of Sintra. Once a favourite of the former royal family, it is now a World Heritage site and a visit had been recommended by everyone I asked. The detour was worthwhile and I enjoyed wandering up and down the village's crooked streets with views of castles and palaces scattered around a green valley. From there it was mostly downhill back to the coast, where I reached the town of Ericeira.

I was now in epic surfers' territory. I spent the night at a place that advertised itself as a surfers hostel, so no wonder I was the only cyclist. Guests were mostly on the young side, with long tousled hair which you could easily lose a comb in; similarly, rooms were spectacularly messy. I guess it was part of the lifestyle. Most of them had been there a month or so and by now treated each other like family. As I arrived at reception Mauricio, the Brazilian owner, was busy checking the next day's wave forecast.

"There's going to be a good swell." he told me, all excited as if I needed large waves to enjoy my bike ride.

He suggested I should store my bike safely in a locked garage full of stacked surfboards until I told him the time of my departure.

"Is that ok? I'll be leaving tomorrow around 8am... 8:30?

He looked at me in dismay and suggested I should fold the bike and keep it in my room.

"Nobody is alive around here before 10 at the earliest..." he said.

One of my roommates was a Dutch guy. He was part of a new breed of millennial hippies whose untidy presence disguised multiple Masters and PhDs. He had been walking El Camino de Campostela in the autumn, escaped the worst of the winter in Faro and was now eager to learn to surf. When I asked how he financed all this leisure time, he casually told me that, when he finds the time, he develops algorithms to automate business contracts registered on a blockchain. Quite a mouthful, but a lucrative one. He said a couple of days with a few hours work here and there was enough to keep him surfing in Ericeira or doing whatever he fancied doing; I felt both envious and happy for him, being still so young yet able to strike a work-life balance that seemed to me just about perfect. From Ericeira to Santa Cruz the waves got bigger and bigger. Scattered in the distance were lots of black dots, belly-down surfers waiting patiently for the right wave to come. I loved the waves. I often stopped just to admire their power as they rolled into perfect tunnels before disintegrating into white foam with a roaring thud. The cycle route took me on a pleasant detour. It followed a dirt road coasting the Lagoa de Óbidos, a shallow lagoon with perfectly still waters which were a complete contrast to the big waves and rough seas of Praia da Foz do Arelho, a few miles away, right by the ocean. An unfriendly wind was against me for most of the day, making for a rough ride that needed pedalling even when descending.

Nearby Nazaré was the ultimate location and one of the sport's Meccas. It was regularly in the news for breaking new records, like the one achieved by a Brazilian named Rodrigo Koxa who, just a year earlier, had surfed a wave over 80 feet tall, a mere 25 metres. Once I got there I couldn't resist walking across the road and sitting on the sandy beach to just stare at the enormous power of the ocean. Waves larger than I had ever seen came smashing in at formidable speed, forming clouds of mist and salty sprays. They crashed one after another with a boom sound that felt like an explosion. No wonder a friend of mine later told me how he had been there in the eighties for a whole month in the summer when he never dared going for a swim. Out of Nazaré I saved myself a first steep hill by boarding the tram rail that climbs from the centre of the modern town to the old upper part called Sitio. Before starting another day of cycling, I headed straight to the famous lighthouse of Praia de Norte, the very spot where world class surfers tackle the biggest waves on earth. The morning swell for that day was forecast at a mere twelve metres, but even that was impressive. I sat down by the wall of Sao Miguel's Fort, next to the red lighthouse, certainly the best seat to contemplate such an amazing spectacle of nature. A handful of motorised water skis were skilfully manoeuvring around giant swells, toeing out a few very mad and very brave surfers and rescuing those that needed rescuing. There wcrc plenty of stories of close calls, with people needing resuscitation, yet allegedly nobody ever died surfing in Nazaré, or so everybody was proud to say. Given their power it was either a blatant lie or a testament to the skills of those that dared to try. As I was watching, a poor chap started off well and with great style before being completely swept off his feet, disappearing into a cloud of foam to not be seen again for a good couple of minutes. It looked both inspiring and scary. I could have spent a whole day sitting on that wall but I had to get going. A cycleway as good as any I had experienced revealed views of long sandy beaches and yet more big waves. I then moved away from the coast. I followed a road with a series of endless, soul destroying straights that made me wish there was an equivalent of an autopilot for cyclists. I realised that my plan to get to Coimbra before nightfall was unrealistic. I had reserved an accommodation there, but with fifty kilometres still to go, a nasty headwind and half an hour of daylight left, I needed an alternative. With the helping hand of Providence, I spotted a railway line. It was not going to Coimbra, but a couple of friendly railway workers pointed me to an intersection only ten minutes away and told me I could easily make the 5:15 train. The shorter winter days seemed a good excuse for a bit of cheating and a little less cycling.

    I had planned to move temporarily inland thanks to a Portuguese cyclist who advised me to avoid the coastal cycle route section north of Figuera da Foz, which apparently was a sandy nightmare. He was also the one that had told me I shouldn't miss Coimbra, which he said was one of the nicest Portuguese cities. Half a morning was spent cycling around this historic city whose most famous buildings are set on top of a hill, part of a university complex that is one of the most prestigious in the country. The road out of Coimbra joined the Portuguese Camino, a less known variant of the traditional French and Spanish routes; it starts from Lisbon and heads North to Compostela. I passed quite a few pilgrims during the day, armed with patience, faith and walking sticks. For lunch I indulged in a traditional *cocido*, a mix of boiled meats and vegetables that is always served in epic portions. The waiter emphasised that it is pork meat but not that fatty. In reality, with pigs ears and trotters thrown in, it was as fatty a meal as I could manage and it took me a good few hours to properly digest it. Thankfully I was at least cycling and burning off most of it. After a few hours I rejoined the coast at Gafanha de Nazaré searching for a suitable place to pitch my tent, probably for the last time given that I was only a night away from Porto, my final destination. After Torreira the cycleway, once again meticulously marked, entered a vast pine forest, and I rode along stretches of raised wooden boards and miniature bridges that only added to the enjoyment. Early morning sun beams shone sideways, piercing through the tall trees like streams of light in a church's nave. On a more prosaic note, this section of woods also seemed to attract prostitutes and their clients which I thought particularly odd at 10 o' clock in the morning. Some of them even wished me a good day. At Espinho I started feeling the buzz of a big city getting closer.

- Porto, PORTUGAL -

The cycleway stuck to the coastline, following miles and miles of raised wooden walkways that kept me clear of sand dunes that are constantly shifting, exposed to the strong winds. I wondered about the patience and care needed to build them; the workers must have had patience in spades, probably even more than the Camino walkers. Porto was no Nazaré, but before turning right and following the Rio Douro into the city centre, the Atlantic put on one last wave show for me. Gratefully I stopped and admired it. Vila Nova de Gaia appeared in front of me, with its crooked streets, old buildings and all its famous Port wineries. There was one last push up a steep hill in order to reach the ramps of Ponte Dom Luis and enter the city in style.

I arrived as my odometer clocked one thousand kilometres cycled in Portugal. Two weeks of uninterrupted sun, something I had hardly experienced in summer and would never have expected in winter, and in a country so exposed to the unpredictable moods of the Atlantic. It isn't always like that, as I heard. A German couple living in Porto told me how just the previous year, at the same time, it had been raining constantly for weeks. The final day was spent mostly walking the streets of Porto: it seemed to me the nicest city I had seen in the country, rich in history and with surprises behind each corner. 'Azulejos' houses, palaces and churches had their front faces covered in white tiles decorated with exquisite blue line drawings and patterns. By the river were the rickety houses of the historic quarter of Ribeiro, tinted in striking pastel colours that were a treasure trove for any wannabe photographer. Sightseeing boats filled with tourists paced up and down the river. I felt blessed strolling the wide walkways along the Rio Douro, a warm sun still shining and the tall metal girders of the Luiz bridge sparkling.

* * *

Turkish Delight

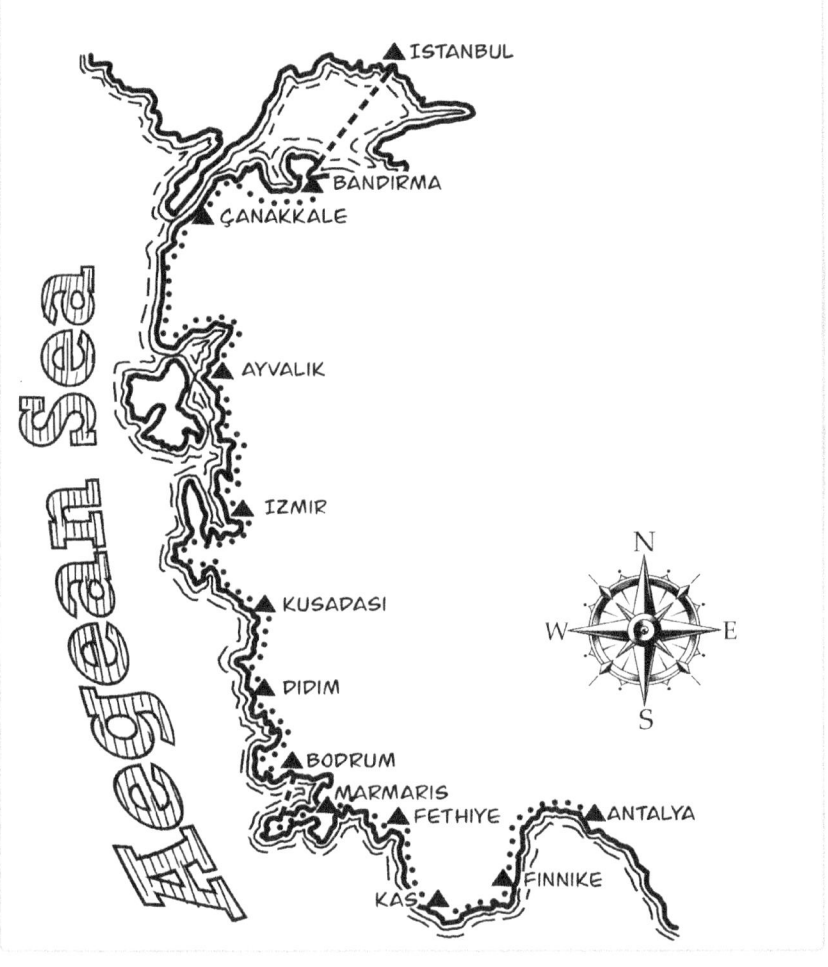

Turkish Delight

Istanbul sits astride two continents, one foot firmly in Europe, the other crossing over into Asia. With its glorious past and unique geographical position, one is stunned by its chaos yet charmed by its beauty. Sitting in the gardens of Sülemaniye mosque whose white stones are bathed in a hazy morning light, I savour some of the peace that the busy city seems to have forgotten. The mosque sits on top of a hill overlooking the bay where the sun is rising, lighting sparkles on the waters of the Bosphorus Strait. I had waited a long time to visit this country that, thanks to the hospitality of its people, its affordable prices and natural beauty, is a favourite amongst travellers and cyclists.

Half a day was enough to part company with Istanbul's public transport. Advertised on billboards as tourist-friendly and convenient, it turned out to be anything but. An afternoon was spent trying and failing to buy an *Istanbul kart*, the card that the leaflets had told me was the best way to explore the city. Although necessary to travel on trains, buses and ferries, even with the kind help of local commuters, there seemed to be no easy way to purchase one. Cash was inserted into modern looking machines, the right buttons were pressed on my behalf, yet all I got was an error message in Turkish. Machines did not accept credit cards, could not be bothered to return change and seemed extremely fussy about the notes one used. Transactions at several stations inevitably failed; to make me feel better, those who tried to help told me that they also found it frustrating at times. This would have not been a big deal if there was a manned ticket office somewhere but there were none. The system's obvious hiccups were taken advantage of by enterprising individuals who were always there when a tourist needed them. They at least did carry an Istanbul Kart and had figured out that letting troubled tourists through gates asking for the most expensive fare was a viable business. A few times I gave in to their services as they let me through the barriers illegally and ticketless. For the first time in my life, despite years of independent travel, I longed for a guide with a raised umbrella or a flag who could escort me around safely.

A thousand miles of cycling awaited me but after these public transport failures this journey had to be started on foot. Istanbul's chaotic traffic was not meant for cyclists and I wanted the freedom to visit all sites without having to worry about the bike. With a few illegal journeys on trains, and lots of walking, I managed to visit some of the city's main sights, getting at least a small taste of it. For convenience, I had reserved a room at a guest house in Yenikapi. This was a stone's throw away from the ferry which, in a couple of days, would be taking me across to Bandirma on the Asian side, ready to begin cycling. I arrived early in the afternoon. I rang the doorbell, knocked and waited a short while; a little girl, five at most, opened the door ajar and peered through it, gauging whether I should be allowed in or not. She must have trusted me. She let me in and pointed to an armchair by the entrance, inviting me to sit down while she confidently started a series of phone calls. During the last one there was some serious scolding from the voice on the other side. The poor little girl listened patiently, raising her eyes and with a smirk on her face; she was not quite convinced that in a metropolis of almost twenty million inhabitants putting so much trust in a foreigner with a folding bicycle could be risky. In a matter of minutes Ydiamin arrived and after more telling off and a few minutes to calm his nerves down, he welcomed me with a big smile and the whitest teeth I had ever seen.

Half a day strolling around the city was enough to realise that cosmetic surgery was big business in this country. Not only were teeth whitened; hordes of tourists as well as locals had their noses straightened, hair transplanted, lips filled plump and cheeks properly sculpted. As a result, I encountered an unusually high percentage of

- Istanbul, TURKEY -

people with bandaged noses, scalps that were bloody yet still quite bald, and stitched up faces, as if they were fresh from a fist fight; it gave the impression that I had ended up in a very dangerous and violent place. Conversely, it seemed a paradise for pet lovers; stray cats and dogs were everywhere, but well taken care of by the citizens, who walked about carrying bags of pet food and water in order to refill inexhaustible bowls. Neighbourhoods competed in kindness by building the best dog houses and the most attractive shelters for cats.

With much cycling planned, all I had time for was a few of Istanbul's must-dos and must-sees. There were lots of mosques including the iconic Hagia Sophia, the world famous bazaars selling all kinds of goods and spices, the Basilica's Cistern and the Topkapi Palace with all its luxury and grandeur, showing off the power that was once held by the Ottoman Empire. Surprisingly, despite such a glorious history of mighty Sultans and epic conquests, modern times had been hijacked by the ever present image of Atatürk, the revolutionary founding father of the Republic of Turkey. He must have been in a league of his own I thought. His stern face with the immaculately groomed moustache was plastered and printed on every possible surface; he had a total monopoly on banknotes, which made me wonder what the great Sultan Mehmet would have made of it all; despite all the sword fighting and the spilt blood, his face didn't even make it onto a fiver.

I had been warned to avoid cycling out of Istanbul due to the city's atrocious traffic, so I boarded a ferry for a much safer passage to the Asian shore and the town of Bandirma. I broke a personal record in carelessness, realising as soon as I had boarded that I must have packed a bike with a tyre puncture. I thought the two-hour journey would be a convenient time to fix it; however, health and safety prevented passengers from standing on the outer deck where the bike had to be parked. On board I met a rather silent Texan guy called Raz who had cycled all the way from Holland and was now only a week away from ending his tour in the city of Izmir. Once we arrived we said goodbye, as he was spending the night in Bandirma while I had to find a quiet corner with some shade to fix my wheel and get started. Given his light racing bike and knotty calves and thighs I was pretty sure it wouldn't take him long to overtake me anyway.

I started cycling along what could well have been the emergency lane of a motorway; plenty of space was given to me by the large lorries which accounted for most of the sparse traffic and I felt very safe in a country with a reputation for bad driving. I quickly learnt that it was neither traffic nor poor driving I had to watch out for but rather close encounters with Anatolian shepherd dogs and Kangals. I had read enough reports from other cyclists about some amusing close calls and the odd accident. The warning was clear: Turkish dogs in the countryside are always large, have an irritable nature and are not to be taken lightly. Farmers as well as shepherds are leaving them unleashed and free to do what they're best at, guarding territory and chasing foreign cyclists. They were nothing like the meek lot I had got used to in Istanbul, gentrified by the quantities of food left by strangers to the point of having forgotten how to bark. These in the countryside were larger than a good-sized German shepherd, had a fat and rather mean face and were definitely stroppy. Combined with the fact that, outside urban areas, seeing a bicycle seemed a rare occurrence I was bound to be tested and it did not take me long to learn from first hand experience!

I was cruising along the side of a motorway with multiple lanes, hardly the place one expects to be suddenly chased by a fierce beast, but at a certain point I must have passed too close to the border of a large farm. An almighty barking started down the bank of the road and a quick glance to my right was enough to see that a sizeable dog was sprinting towards me, upset as if Genghis Khan was about to invade and take over the whole place. As if one was not enough, all the barking aroused two more dogs a little further on; they also sprinted towards me, ready to get involved and join forces. Past experience in other countries had taught me that outrunning them can be futile at best and with some bad luck can be the worst of mistakes. I thought I should test my main strategy, loosely borrowed from Gandhi. I stopped and addressed all that fierceness and aggression with its opposite: with gentle words and a lot of faith and hope that this ought to work even in Turkey. The Kangal dog was confused by such a wimp reaction and didn't quite know how to take it; just in case, it kept on barking and gave me a good display of sharp teeth that, if not as white as those that I had seen parading in the city, were not something I wanted to feel in my heels or calves. I moved away slowly, pushing my bike to one side, hoping that Gandhi was right and wouldn't leave me disappointed; the dog followed close right behind me, sniffing my legs and barking as if there was no tomorrow; time seemed to have come to a complete stop and two minutes felt like eternity. After a few miles of this he must have realised I was either a coward or not as mean as I had first appeared: the barking slowly faded; *Ahimsa* had worked its wonders even in faraway Turkey.

I reached a tiny fishing village at twilight, a little shaken and hungry. It had a single restaurant that looked rather busy for a Monday night. Guests were exclusively Turkish and as I sat down for dinner some of them attempted to talk to me only to realise that their efforts were wasted. I used my translation app and, helped by hand gestures, I conveyed that I was from Italy and was heading to the southern city of Antalya. There were no menus but everyone sat at their tables looking extremely happy with what they had been given. The elderly owner was bubbly and of a gentle nature. Not having a menu to point at, it all felt hopeless and those that tried to help me eventually gave up and ordered for me: Fried calamari came as a starter, followed by a mixed salad, and the main dish was a white fish cooked in a creamy sauce. Everything tasted delicious and came in generous portions, and all I could do was smile and give a thumbs up to whoever had decided for me. Bicycles often bring one to the most unexpected of places; a chance encounter with strangers in a restaurant with no name in a forlorn little port can produce some of the fondest memories. The summer well over, it was getting dark sooner than I had thought. I had to get going and asked the owner for the bill, clueless as to where I would spend the night. He asked something in Turkish which I assumed to be 'where are you going?'

"I have a tent." I replied, trusting the translation on my phone.

He pointed at a covered gazebo in the restaurant garden and said I was welcome to put my tent there if I wanted. Given the quality of the meal and my lack of knowledge when it comes to fish, I was curious about the final price of such a sumptuous dinner that I had not ordered. In some places around the world, and I sadly include my own country, with a little bad luck they would have set me up with lobsters, truffles and whatever took their fancy. Not here. The kind owner showed me a total on his calculator which was so inexpensive that I first thought it might be the gazebo's nightly fee. It turned out that that was the grand total and the gazebo was complimentary.

I left early in the morning, the restaurant still closed. I followed a tiny road out of the village that slowly lost its tarmac and turned to soil. With fields and farms all around me I remembered the experience of the previous day and felt jittery. The white furry faces and black noses of two stray Anatolian stuck out from the tall grass checking whether I would take the wrong turn. With nerves as tight as the strings of a mandolin I kept cycling, as alert as an antelope on the Savannah plains. Eventually I rejoined the main road and had the wide emergency lane all to myself as trucks loaded to the brim sped past me. I stopped at a café where three customers were sipping coffee on the veranda. Finding out I was Italian, one of them pointed his finger at me and excitedly shouted: "Meloni! Meloni!"
For a moment I thought he was trying to sell me some melons, a popular fruit in Turkey, but he was in fact referring to the newly elected Italian Prime Minister from the extreme right party. I hadn't really caught up on the latest news and my lack of excitement left him rather disappointed.

In Gürecealti I rejoined the coast feeling as if this journey was now just starting. I had almost cycled one hundred kilometres, which felt much harder on a day of headwinds, and found myself again wondering where I would end up spending the night. The map showed a promising campsite before the town of Lapseki. I soon reached it, but as it turned out it was only a restaurant. Nevertheless I noticed it had a quiet garden at the back and, emboldened by the previous night's experience, took out my mobile phone and started typing.....

"I have a tent. If I have dinner can I sleep in the garden?"

The text was too tiny for the owner's eyesight, so he left and returned with a pair of glasses to make sense of it.

"No problem", he said, so naturally as if it was something that happened most nights.

I was also hoping for a shower, though, and tried to explain by means of clumsy hand gestures and some bad acting.

"Douche?" he asked, with a French pronunciation, though I later learnt this was the word for shower in Turkish.

"No problem" he said, once again.

He led me along a series of dark corridors at the back of the restaurant and showed me a shabby but perfectly working shower that I was free to use. It always comes as a surprise to find that, at times, life in what we call 'less' developed countries turns out to be much simpler. Another free night meant ordering another hefty meal, which is never a bad proposition after a long day of cycling. They piled up the barbecued lamb, the chicken skewers, the dips and a mountain of french fries, and I wondered if it might be the first tour ever where I ended up fatter than I started. The evening turned lively as a group that was sitting at the corner table took out a violin and a *bendir*, the traditional Turkish equivalent of hand drums, and started passionately singing some traditional folk songs.

    The Imam at the local mosque started testing speakers for any malfunction before the ceremonies at sunrise. In the morning, I left without saying goodbye as there were no signs of life at the restaurant after what had surely been a late night. I was heading towards Çanakkale, along the familiar emergency lane, looking forward to taking a turn thirty kilometres further on, joining the old coastal road which promised to be much quieter and far more scenic. The long straights of the E90 with its repetitive climbs and descents seemed never ending at my snail's speed, and good progress was hampered by a blistering headwind. To get out of a stretch of boredom, I mentally rehearsed some Turkish, hoping it would spice up some future conversations. Good morning was *günaydin*, afternoon *tünaydin*, *ekmek* was bread and *süt* was milk. When I needed water I asked for *su* and once I reached a town I knew I needed to follow signs saying *sehir merkezi,* and then would end up in the city centre. To endear me to people in case of needing help or for any emergency, there was *Türkiye Harika,* Turkey is great, or the ultimate people pleaser, *Atatürk'ü seviyorum,* I love Ataturk. To end any conversation, *Türkçemi bitirdim* worked nicely: I have run out of Turkish.

A couple of hours of boring roads worked wonders. By the time I reached Çanakkale and met Dogân and his girlfriend, my hosts for the night, I was eager to put it all into practice:

"Memnun oldum!"
"Benim adim Gianni, İtalya'dan geliyorum, Antalya'ya dönüyorum"
"Wifi var mi?"

Nice to meet you, my name is Gianni, I come from Italy, I am cycling to Antalya and - the all important and ultimate necessity - do you have wifi?

Despite the atrocious pronunciation I think I was understood or at least I provoked some laughter.

Happy to have left the main roads behind me, I followed a narrow coastal road that was the first Turkish attempt at creating a cycleway I had seen; albeit a rather half-hearted attempt, limited to a stripe of blue paint colouring the tarmac on the sideway. Here were the first views of pristine alcoves and tempting beaches, but I held out for that first swim. The Sea of Marmara got narrower and narrower, turning into the Dardanelles Strait before opening up into the wide open waters of the Aegean Sea. I was close to the ancient city of Troy whose exact location is unknown; this explained the multitude of signposts pointing to it in all directions and contradicting each other. If they were all to be believed Troy was just about everywhere!   I had even seen a life-size replica of the Trojan horse in the city centre of Çanakkale, apparently a movie prop, and all that remained of a Brad Pitt Hollywood blockbuster. I felt blessed by the warm sun, and it still felt like summer; I had to move inland, on a road that turned out to be an ancient Roman Way with the original bumpy cobblestones, definitely not meant for bicycles. The landscape changed to open farmland, where women bent double were picking peppers and tomatoes. They put all my efforts and the odd complaints into perspective; here they were, with no choice in this back-breaking work picking fruit and vegetables, while I was moaning about a bumpy road and headwinds. Scattered on top of the hills all around me were wind turbines, their huge steel blades spinning frantically, generating energy while I seemed to suffer from a lack of it.

Once back at the coast I spotted one of the first campsites: Agora it was called, and it appropriately welcomed me with the loud barking of an Anatolian shepherd dog in a foul mood. Why do they all hate cyclists, I wondered? I faced up to my fears and by the time I made it through to reception, he calmed down and turned into a pretty tame dog; I stopped and, as he seemed to enjoy the smells from a day of sweaty cycling, I was about to pat him gently on the head.

"Don't touch him! He'll bite you..." said the girl unequivocally.

It didn't seem a good idea to have an aggressive dog roaming freely around a public campsite, but here it seemed perfectly acceptable and no one made a fuss about it; in fact there were three large dogs roaming freely, taking their turns at frightening guests. At night I had to postpone going to the restrooms for a pee. Hardly had I moved out of my tent with my bright torch shining when I heard the first few growlings. The Anatolian was half asleep not far from my tent and it seemed that toilets were very much part of his territory so I thought I had better hold it. In the morning we were friends again; I bribed him with some pieces of bread and a handful of crisps and he allowed me to walk all the way to the toilets unescorted. I sat at a table writing a few pages in my diary with a friendly black stray cat sitting on my lap purring and the Anatolian lying lazily at my feet . Nobody needs pets in Turkey…

Every now and then I traded good roads for the faster highways. Beside offering speed, these were also excellent stretches to enjoy some of the sweetest and ripest figs. With traffic fast moving and everyone eager to get somewhere quickly, there was a bounty of fruits that could be easily picked from fully loaded trees. I stopped for lunch in the busy farming village of Geyikli, watching a steady stream of people try their luck at gambling. They queued patiently to buy scratch cards and used the side of a coin to carefully reveal yet another disappointment. Some were clearly addicted and were soon back, rejoining the queue. I wondered what winning the jackpot would look like: given the unconditional love and respect he enjoys in the country, probably scratching the card to uncover one more stern image of Ataturk.

I had reached a part of the Turkish coast that is steeped in Greek history. In Gülpinar, right on top of a steep hill, I visited the temple of Apollo Smintheion. It is mentioned in the Iliad, or so I was told by the large signboard in front of it, not pretending to have read even a page of it. As a student I had a remarkable lack of interest for old civilisations and history; and only as I grew older did I start to find some meaning and appreciation for everything ancient. Further on along the same road was Behramkale or ancient Assos - but it was also known as Apollonia, which might have confused ancient travellers as much as it still confuses tourists following satellite maps. I discovered that Aristotle lived here for a while and founded one of his Academies. What remains today is a pretty village taken over by stalls of vendors selling trinkets and souvenirs mostly made in China. I walked up to the hilltop and the temple of Athena whose ruins overlook the bay, with the Greek island of Lesbos just a stone's throw away. Later, I was back on the main road for about an hour, until I noticed that a little road by the sea was drawn on my map; surely, that must be more interesting.

It was, in the sense that after a few kilometres, having passed a few houses, it shed all its tarmac and turned rocky and bumpy before taking me straight into a muddy swamp. I am not someone who enjoys getting unnecessarily dirty if I can help it, but I had cycled too far to backtrack so I pushed on, reluctantly, eventually emerging in an olive grove. Most unsuitable for cycling, I pushed the bike whilst trying to keep positive, reminding myself that if I had lost a road I had at least found the sea that sparkled on my right side. A rocky path was followed by a dusty road that led me straight into a full blown building site. A disastrous bit of cycling planning then turned worse, as I had to find my way through cranes, portaloos and builders sweating and possibly swearing. Definitely not the kind of Turkish experience one sees advertised in pamphlets. Interestingly, I was not the only foreigner who had lost his way. In my travelling experience there is always a German where you least expect them. In fact two. I caught up with an elderly couple with large rucksacks, wooden walking sticks and all kinds of trinkets dangling; they hardly spoke any English. I guessed they must have been well into their seventies, and I understood that they had left Germany determined to walk all the way to Jerusalem. They seemed unphased and happy and surely trusted more in faith than I did. Meeting them somehow made me feel a little better in myself though; I realised that I was not alone and that some were suffering at an even slower pace. I eventually reached a single track road and a seaside village with a small beach that seemed just right to wipe away some of the dust and indulge in that very first swim.

There was nothing to complain about along the old coastal road to Izmir. Being narrow and a little bumpy for cars it had hardly any traffic and took me through some interesting villages, up and down hills thick with olive trees, with wonderful vistas over the sea often opening up in front of me. I admit to having a bit of a stubborn nature. Before Denizköy, while looking at my maps, I had noticed a shortcut that went steeply downhill and reached the same village that on the main road involved further climbing before a long descent. By now I should have known better and distrusted Turkish shortcuts, but I followed my cyclist's gut feeling and convinced myself that going downhill is much better. After an initial steep descent on tarmac I was met by fences and a gate. There were some notices and signposts in Turkish but, too lazy to pick up my phone and guess a possible translation, I decided to ignore them. Instead, I spotted a passage by the side where the fence was torn open and kept going. Half way down the mountain it turned into a rocky trail until I had almost reached the beach. Almost, in the sense that I was met by a second gate and fencing that this time was much more sturdy and impeccably maintained. A large padlock and some barbed wire ensured that I would not easily get through it. I reluctantly thought there was no option but to retreat and walk all the way back up the mountain, but on the other side was an attractive beach with its little campsite.

A man was standing at a kiosk so I started shouting and waving to draw his attention. At first he completely ignored me but once again Turkish hospitality soon kicked in and he came to my rescue. The fence was reasonably high but the man was as large as a wardrobe and stretched his arms up high, suggesting I could pass my luggage and bike to him and then attempt to climb it. The gate was rather wobbly under my weight but I scrambled up and down, far from elegantly but at least without scratches. I thanked him and to show my gratitude, insisted on joining him at the kiosk for a drink and an ice cream. There was the usual back and forth with our mobile phones translating English sentences into Turkish, which he then conveyed to his wife behind the counter. When I said I was going to Antalya he said something lengthy to her with a smirk and they burst out laughing. They probably agreed that if I kept trespassing and having to climb locked gates as I just did, I would never make it. After a week of headwinds I put all my hopes in the forecast that was promising a change in direction. It turned out to be most accurate. I woke up and began another day's cycling with a strong southerly tailwind. I was making fast progress along an emergency lane, without the need for much pedalling, thanking Mother Nature's helping hand that finally benefited cyclists as well as wind turbines.

- Kozbeyli, TURKEY -

The original plan involved reaching the town of Foça, but I stopped short, finding accommodation at the historic village of Kozbeyli. I had reserved a nice room with a view over the bay and I thought I should make the most of it and enjoy it at leisure. The property owner had advertised her place skilfully, claiming the village was one of the best kept secrets of the Aegean, which sounded a bit over promising. The room, right at the top of a three storey house that overlooked the tiny village, was indeed bright and the views were excellent. Ayse was a welcoming host and spoke good English. She had escaped the crazy hustle and bustle of Istanbul, where she was born, to retire somewhere quieter, rent out a couple of rooms for income and write poetry. She had obviously put to good use her skills when describing the village, which indeed had a picturesque location overlooking the bay and a few old houses worth looking at, but was otherwise verging on the decrepit. As I had arrived in the main square, there had been some Turkish tourists passing though and even a couple of small buses coming and going. The main attraction was a few minutes walk down a narrow path below the house I was staying in. It was a minute old mosque dating back to the eleventh century. I walked to the front terrace where a man was sitting on the bench by the entrance as if he had been waiting for me. He smiled and looked friendly, so I sat down next to him admiring the distant views over the sea. As he spoke just Turkish we relied on technology; typing and translating and showing each other's phone screens we managed to have at least a basic conversation. He turned out to be the village Imam, which allowed me to finally get an answer to a question that had intrigued me ever since visiting my first Muslim country. Nothing philosophical about the Quran teachings but rather something very practical. I typed it on the phone:

"Are the calls to prayer that wake me up every morning live or are they pre-recorded?"

He didn't seem to mind my silly question but he was obviously also keen to make a point.

"I DO THEM…" he typed with his thumb and in capital letters.

With his hand he then gestured I should follow him. We entered the mosque, walking barefoot on soft carpets until we reached a corner where there was a wooden cabinet and a microphone stand. He opened a door and revealed an example of those hifi systems that woke me up most mornings and which I had since learnt to dread. It was a full blown system with multiple stacks that allowed the creation of all kinds of ethereal, special effects. I suppose chance meant that I had turned up in time for prayers, or maybe he just wanted to show me that he was in charge and that he could do it, if he ever wanted to; he flicked a switch and pointed to the microphone to make sure I kept quiet and then launched into a beautiful call to prayer, broadcast via a network of speakers that reached the most hidden corners of the valley. Unlike the morning versions, which seemed always to come far too early and at times scared me, I was growing fond of these afternoon and evening prayers and this was one to remember.

I left Kozbeyli on an overcast morning that kept the sun hidden until around midday. Dull light does not only transform landscapes, it plays havoc with my mood too; I cycled along thinking it would be nicer if the sun was shining. The road followed the contour of the seashore and I had at least the wind on my side, with gusts that pushed me all the way to Foça. The sun came out just in time for my visit to one of the nicest towns so far. By the harbour a fisherman was untangling his large nets and transferring the day's catch into polystyrene boxes under the loving gaze of half a dozen cats. Experience had taught them that some of the fish sizes would not cut it for the market and so they waited patiently, aware that sooner or later their time would come. Before too long there were two open boxes laid on the floor full of fresh fish, only a few metres away from their noses, but there was a silent agreement so they just waited; the fisherman must have felt like a bliss bestowing God to them, and should never be betrayed. In a side street, the local market was buzzing with locals sifting through piles of colourful clothes and large cases of ripe melons, tomatoes and peppers. A policeman was having a bad day; he was shouting to the crowds hoping to find the owner of a van that had been conveniently parked right in the middle of a one way street, grounding all traffic to a halt.

Getting into Izmir, roughly half way through my journey, was a little messy with heavier traffic and I got a little lost along the way. I made it just as my front tyre decided it was about time to get a puncture and with a steady hiss started slowly deflating. Izmir is the third largest city in the country. I spent an afternoon walking around the quarter of Alsancak, Konak and Kemeralti's vast market;

everywhere was fizzing with people and excitement. Small shops full of characters competed in offering bargains, drawing crowds of locals and tourists disembarking from giant cruise ships. Everything that could possibly be wanted could be found here. On the other hand, entire streets were devoted to a particular interest or subject with shops selling pretty much the same things. I walked along a street dedicated exclusively to maths textbooks. Surely an interesting place for shoppers, but a bit less so for a cyclist whose bags are packed full of necessities and have no space left for bargains.

Leaving Izmir was much easier than arriving. I simply followed the wonderful cycle route along the coast that took me all the way out of the city without having to deal with any of its traffic. I figured out it is an unofficial continuation of Eurovelo 8, the Mediterranean Way, that I had followed a year earlier from Barcelona to Italy. The official route ends in Athens but there is an extension project that, with a ferry transfer to a couple of Greek islands, reaches Turkey and then ends up in Cyprus. This was part of it. A steady, northerly breeze blessed me like a sailor with full wind in his sails. Despite having planned to do half as much, in order to include a stop for a swim, I ended up cycling over a hundred kilometres in a day for the first time on this trip. Winds made the sea rather choppy so there wasn't much chance of a dip. I went through Sigacik, another picture perfect village with white painted houses with dangling bougainvillaea in flowers. I kept going, hoping to find a good spot for the tent. During the day I saw plenty of good spots to put the tent but I felt as if it was always too early. Outside the town of Seferihisar the light was too dim to continue safely so I took a turn off the main road and climbed a rocky trail up to a barren hill. As the sun dropped behind the mountain, the same wind that had helped me when cycling turned blustery as I struggled to pitch the tent without losing it, on what felt like the windiest hill in Turkey.

The tent proved sturdy enough to survive the strong gusts that battered it all night. I packed it carefully just before sunrise with the help of large rocks to keep it from taking off in the sky. I walked down the hill and was back on the road as blinding low rays of sun enveloped the landscape in a yellow hue. As I descended a cloud of thin dust was rising up from the valley. I realised I was approaching a large farm where a shepherd was busy gathering his flock, ready to set off roaming. Alarm bells started ringing. I thought a fierce dog in a foul mood was bound to be waiting for me around the next bend. I started braking to take it slowly and just as the farm was in full view across the road the chase started. I stopped and got off the bike immediately, while not one but seven dogs surrounded me barking as if I was a rebellious lamb. The fiercest one, and leader of the pack, wore a metal collar with spikes that made him look like my worst nightmare. It was all back to Gandhi's playbook. I played the friendly card, saying good morning to them in my gentlest tone, but this time it did not seem to be working.

The shepherd was just across the road and, seeing what was happening, started shouting and beating his long stick, half upset with the dogs, half with me; I had definitely turned up uninvited and at the worst time. A couple of Turkish people, speaking good English, stopped with their car and lowered their windows to ensure I was alright. I told them that with a bit of luck I should be. As soon as I tried to take a few steps to move away the dogs encircled me again and barked like mad. Luckily they seemed to limit their aggression to looking terrifying and sniffing my legs. The shepherd lost his patience; he sprinted across the road beating his stick and making a big scene, which agitated me further but somehow calmed the dogs! He spoke some Turkish which I took to mean "get on your bloody bike and disappear from here" which I willingly did! After such a stressful departure I pined for a relaxing swim.

The best beaches were yet to come and the further south I travelled the more I found. Looking down from the road I spotted Kargacik Koyu, an attractive cove with a restaurant and a campsite. The season was over and it was closed, but I met the owner who was sitting at a table chatting with a friend. His name was Meli and he had worked as a dentist for forty years in Zürich. Now retired, he had returned to this little corner of paradise in his own country. He asked whether I was cycling around Turkey and said I was welcome to stop, swim and take a shower; having asked him whether there was any food, he said that if I waited thirty minutes it would be ready and I could join him. When it was time to say goodbye it proved impossible to pay for anything other than the beer I had had. Selçuk and its famous archeological site of Ephesus was nearby and it was the right time to get off the bike and spend a leisurely day and a half sightseeing. Back on the bike, I reached buzzing Kusadasi, very much a resort city on the main tourist trail. There, I could find all kinds of comforts and conveniences while losing a little of the real Turkey. Thereafter the tourists disappeared and Turkey was back again once more in Soke, just twenty kilometres across the mountain and too far from the sea to have enough appeal. The difference was quite striking and it felt as if I had just moved through two different countries.

- Ephesus, TURKEY -

"You don't have to go to Soke, there's nothing there." Meli had told me.

What he didn't realise is that going through ordinary places is very much part of a cycling journey and provides glimpses of real life in a country. There was certainly much more of that in Soke than there was in Kusadasi. Having acquired a bit of a tan I was frequently mistaken for a local and asked for directions. More phrases had to be learnt: "Türkçe konuşmuyorum", I don't speak Turkish, was easy enough to remember and just about perfect in most situations. Roads varied from boring straights that seemed to last a lifetime to the most entertaining single lanes twisting through olive groves. Descents had to be earned as always; I started a gruelling climb out of Akbuk that ended up being a mixture of cycling and walking up some pretty steep ramps. Once in Gürçamlar I took a diversion in order to spend the night at a farm campsite by the coast. The friendly owner was most welcoming and when asked about the price he was charging he seemed almost embarrassed and decided on the hoof. Four Euros is all he wanted for a tent space and hot shower and with another four I could have dinner with him and his three friends that were visiting from Ankara. Before that, a deserted beach was within walking distance and I managed a last swim in pristine waters just before sunset.

I don't want to spoil the dreams of those who want to give up the noise of the city to find peace and quiet in the countryside, but it does not always work out that way, at least not on a Saturday night. As it was getting darker the farmer's son turned on his powerful hifi system and revelled in his own rave party. Loud beats of techno music shattered the silence, with bass frequencies so deep that they messed with my brain until short of midnight. Dogs' ears must have also suffered. When he switched it off the stray dogs vented their frustration in bouts of barking that kept the night alive. Eventually their throats must have gone a little sore as the barking dwindled. I counted how many dogs were left. Three...two...one....there was a clear winner for the night, a dog that kept ranting as if there was no tomorrow; he wasn't satisfied with mere victory, he wanted to humiliate the rest of them. He kept at it relentlessly, for an encore that lasted half an hour before collapsing in total exhaustion with laryngitis. Finally, I thought...some well deserved rest. Not quite. There is something else typically Turkish that I had experienced earlier on this journey. With nearby Russia and Ukraine at war with each other across the Black Sea, and sharing borders with Iran, Iraq and Syria, Turkey has half of the world's unrest on its door steps. Their answer is a mighty army that annoyingly keeps the most scenic spots in the country off-limits while constantly training for doomsday. Late into the night I was woken by the loud explosions and gunshots of a mock up war in the nearby mountain. To make it feel even more real there were the engine rumbles of two helicopters passing by on a low level flight. I fell asleep briefly, until the Imam put an end to my efforts with a heartfelt rendition of a call to prayer, let down only by the static noise of a speaker system that badly needed repairing.

Fresh from all that rest, the new day started with the longest climb so far. I moved into the province of Mugla, struck by its beautiful green hills thick with forests of pine trees. The road had hardly any traffic and plenty of character and once I made it to the top, it dived down steeply onto a plain of farms and the distant sight of landings at Milas International airport. With good access, nearby Bodrum is one of the most popular tourist destinations in the country. Quite a contrast from the farm stay a day earlier, much busier and just as noisy! Before arriving I stopped for a swim on one of the best beaches I had seen so far. It had its own restaurant but otherwise was empty apart from myself and another guest. Getting into Bodrum, the traffic increased and the road turned into a multi-lane highway. I climbed a couple more hills before diving down, right into the thick of the busy town, joining the large crowd of autumn sunshine seekers. Despite the crowds I quite liked the town. Its location, with hills at the back and the large port making its long sweeping arch around the bay was most attractive. It had something for everyone, the elegant and exclusive restaurants and cocktail bars of the Marina to one side, and the fast food joints and coffee places on the opposite side.

Riding among the tourist hotspots of the Aegean and Mediterranean coast, I had wrongly assumed that in most places there would be some familiarity with spoken English. It turned out very much not to be the case. Communication was at times a challenge, yet I quite liked Turkish people's unique attitude to learning English. I had a feeling that fundamentally, they just could not be bothered learning it while the rest of the world strives to learn it. I had noticed this lack of enthusiasm even in cosmopolitan Istanbul. The general attitude is that this is Turkey and the Turkish language is what is spoken. Whether one likes it or not there are two options: visitors can go through the pain of trying to learn it, or else they can rely completely on their phones' ability to translate it. Days before, a farmer, and my host for the night, was not too familiar with modern technology; he rang up a friend in a panic. The person at the other end could string together a few sentences in English, so the mobile was passed back and forth in order to have a basic conversations that hopefully made him feel at ease about the unexpected visit of a foreigner. Later he typed on my phone that Turkish was hard enough for him and that the last thing he wanted was learning a foreign language.

In order to continue my journey I had to take a ferry to Datça, a long thin peninsula that stretches out not far from the Greek islands of Kos and Rhodes. After about an hour I was off the ferry and had planned a short couple of hours ride in order to reach a campsite. The landscape turned to mountains that were taller and sharper than hitherto. I reached my final destination where I was rejected for the first time; even the legendary Turkish hospitality was this time left wanting. It was a large resort with enough security and barriers to make it feel more exclusive than it merited; there were lots of well tended gardens and elegant cottages but very little sympathy for cyclists. I was stopped at the first barrier by a security guard. I told him that I wanted to stay for the night at the campsite. Without giving it much thought he said it was full, which at this time of the year I knew was very unlikely. I played my usual 'tired cyclist' card, looking a little drained and pointing at the bike and all its luggage; it seemed to work at first because he made a quick phone call before shrugging and lifting the barrier.

The place was enormous, and I was sure that it would be possible to give me a couple of empty square metres somewhere. After ten minutes cycling I reached reception, where a not so friendly young girl did not seem to be happy to see a guest in what looked like a half empty campsite. She managed to summon enough enthusiasm to at least look at her computer screen and said that she would book me in for three nights when all I wanted was a one night stay. She looked back at the computer and confirmed that the same space available for three nights was somehow not empty just for one; there was no point in arguing so I moved on, cycling further. I found another posh place where they were still not happy for me to stay but at least let me in their restaurant and fed me; after a quick dip in the sea I resumed cycling up a steep mountain in search of that elusive nice tent pitch which I eventually gave up trying to find, settling for a large slab of concrete next to an empty police cabin.

For the final few days figs were bought at the market. A change in people's attitude, or maybe the simple fact that southern Turkey is a little warmer, meant that what was left hanging on the trees was shrunk and dried up by the scorching sun. I heard in the news that a few days earlier Antalya had broken an all time record for October, with 42 degrees celsius. A blessing for everyone cycling in autumn, but I still hoped that by the time I got there it would be somehow cooler. Descending the mountain from the concrete slab emergency campsite, I felt hungry. I regularly noticed establishments with a sign that said *Kahvalti*. I thought it might mean restaurant, pension or guest house, but I finally looked it up in the dictionary and realised it was Turkish for breakfast and exactly what I needed. At a crossroads with a couple of shops and a few houses I saw the sign again. I did not want to miss another chance so I went through the gate and sat at a table on the covered patio by the garden. There was the good omen of a baker taking out hot loaves of bread from a wood-burning oven.

A few customers were tucking into large plates with satisfaction and gusto.

"Kahvalti" I said, not knowing what I would be getting.

I knew it wouldn't be toast, butter, jam and a coffee. The table was set with a small jug of olive oil, salt, pepper, chilli and cutlery. The baker himself turned up with one of his steaming loaves, followed by his son who was carrying tomatoes, cucumbers and a rocket salad. Next came someone whom I assumed must have been the wife. She served me a tray with a number of small wooden containers on it: there was butter, honey, a selection of soft and hard cheeses, a handful of mysterious concoctions and dips and more types of olives than I thought existed. All the food was clearly fresh produce from the farm, with flavours and fragrances never found at my local supermarket. It was a feast for the eye and palate and the best fuel for another day's cycling.When the bill arrived I had the usual feeling that it was not possible and that they must have forgotten something. On the way out I thanked them and felt like typing something Turkish on my phone:

"*Simdiye kadar yedigim en iyi kahvalti...*" Best breakfast I have ever had.

They all laughed, the master baker touched his heart with the palm of his hand, in the gentle gesture of gratitude that is often seen in Muslim countries. That morning feast kept me going for the rest of the day and all the way to Marmaris, another busy resort in an idyllic setting of bays and islets surrounded by mountains.

Turkey is also gifted with talented barbers. They pride themselves on being the absolute best on the planet and have set up shops in cities the world over. It was time to put one to the test and finally get a proper haircut. I took a seat at a barber that turned out to have an excellent CV and certainly did not lack any confidence. He also came with a pedigree. His dad had been the best barber in

Marmaris, he told me, and used to own a shop by the seaside and cut the hair of many famous politicians and Turkish celebrities. As dad was not around I thought it was not that relevant, but hoped that at least he had introduced his son to the scissors when still young. Just as I took my seat he was also candid enough to inform me that he was just sitting in for a friend of his who owned the place and I guess was the 'real' barber.

"Don't worry!" he said, probably noticing signs of concern on my face.

"I am much better than he is…" he continued.
"You are very lucky I am here today! I usually work at the best five star hotel in Marmaris."

That didn't quite reassure me. I hoped he meant that he worked as a barber in the hotel but for all I knew he might as well have been working in Room Service. It was too late to fidget, anyway, and there is only so much one can do to completely mess up a middle aged man's head. I replied that he was the lucky one. One of the positives of two years of pandemic and regular lockdowns meant that I had got used to cutting my own hair and hadn't visited a barber for over two years. Soon I felt a sense of relief. The young chap could certainly handle a comb and a pair of scissors and was now chopping off hair at a blistering speed.

"Amazing how fast you are…" I commented, wondering what the rush was all about and wishing he would slow down a little to lessen the risk of spilling some blood. In hindsight this was a stupid thing to say to someone who obviously did not need further encouragement.

He clearly took it the wrong way.

"To you this might seem fast, but to me… it's just nothing…"
"Cutting hair is all I have done for twenty years of my life." he said, picking up the pace considerably.

He did a good job, finishing his masterpiece without any injuries, but I guess that wasn't up to his usual five stars service.

"You need ear waxing…" he suggested.

Truth be told, I was just cycling in Turkey and was far from trying to impress anyone or win a beauty contest. Still he had a point.

"Go for it!" I encouraged him.

He switched on a little machine on the counter and in a couple of minutes produced some hot red wax that he spread skilfully in my ears with a wooden spatula. A few minutes later, as the burning sensation subsided, I knew what was coming. With a sudden movement he got hold of it and pulled hard, as if he wanted to walk away with my earlobes, putting an end to fifty years of peaceful hair growth in those most secluded cavities. That was five stars enough for me, but he had not quite finished yet; he dipped a long cotton bud stick into a jug of alcohol and then lit it with a lighter.

What could be next I wondered?

Had he had enough of a long haircutting career and decided to put an end to it all by setting on fire his last paying customer?

They do say quality is in the detail. The flames were all for me, but luckily dispensed in swipes that were fast enough to not set me alight. No chance was left even for the most invisible hair to hide. Once it was all over I breathed a sigh of relief. I smelt of burnt chicken but he had done a remarkable job in making me look about ten years younger, with ears as smooth as those of a new born baby.

To keep me entertained along a relatively boring stretch of countryside I thought I would keep count of Ataturk's images. I reached forty seven before midday. His bliss-bestowing gaze is just about everywhere. On posters, sculptures, tattooed arms, graffiti, bumper stickers, t-shirts, flags and sculptures at roundabouts. Due to a lack of time I had planned to cut two days of cycling which I had read would be rather boring, and mostly on a busy highway. Well groomed and looking somehow respectable, for a handful of euros, I took a little bus journey and was whisked two hundred kilometres away, arriving as fresh as a daisy in Fethiye. Sometimes people wonder why anyone bothers with cycling at all. Surely it is much easier and more efficient to hop on buses and trains, making the most of a foreign holiday? As I see it, the answer is very simple. Most of these memories would never have been written without this most perfect means of transport. In a world obsessed with speed and targets, slowing down reminds that life is the journey itself; too often we look and think about where we want to get to and end up missing most of it. For sure I would have never been able to keep an accurate tally of Ataturk's faces while riding a bus.

When I reached Fethiye's station there was some singing going on accompanied by drums and flutes. As I was assembling the bicycle and organising the luggage, what I had thought was a jolly occasion turned sombre; a bus was about to depart and while the chanting and music continued, two inconsolable women burst into cries, sobbing and tears. One of them nearly fainted and had to be carried to a patch of shade not far from where I was standing. Probably yet another son or daughter had gone, searching for fortune elsewhere. I left town and was soon climbing big hills surrounded by forests with higher mountains on the horizon. Some of the peaks must have reached altitudes above two thousand metres but, luckily, I only had to find my way around them. The landscape turned alpine with plenty of perfect tent pitches, but I did not have enough water or food and was pestered by a chronic lack of time. I had to descend back down to the other side where water and food were plentiful, but I failed to find a suitable campsite. It got too dark to continue so, a little desperate, I played the restaurant card that had been so successful so far. I noticed one of those Turkish breakfast signs at a place otherwise a bit run down. An elderly couple were calling it a day, sitting at a table in their garden in almost complete darkness. I asked whether they would let me put the tent somewhere in their garden, promising I would have breakfast the following morning. Once more I felt welcomed.

"Our home is your home." said the lady in her broken English.

In the morning I sat down on their patio as the couple started preparing breakfast with some excellent teamwork. Another large breakfast to get me started. The table was filled with plates, baskets and saucers; some hot flat bread arrived together with a four eggs omelette, an assortment of cheeses, roasted tomatoes and peppers and twelve saucers containing honey, nuts, jams, olives and mysterious sauces. It took them some time to figure out what they should charge me. I left, happy to have felt so welcomed and safe while hoping that my money had also made their day.

- *Kas, TURKEY* -

I had started my journey in stunning Istanbul, but as far as the cycling was concerned I had kept the best for last. Once I rejoined the coastal road I was granted the best views and the best beaches so far. I met Jeff and Chris, two sporty brothers from California who had started cycling in Izmir. Antalya's beaches are world famous and some of the best in Turkey. The road followed the coastline closely and I could not resist stopping for regular dips in the beautiful sea. I spent a few hours with the two Americans in one of the best coves I had seen thus far. They were on their final day of cycling, while I was moving on further south on my way to Kas. This turned out to be the best coastal town visited so far. While still crowded with tourists, it retained the authentic feel of a lived-in place with an exquisite historic centre, a tiny mosque and lots of picturesque shops, restaurants and houses. From there, the road continued, magnificent and mostly empty of traffic. Just before reaching Finike, I glanced down to where a series of wood-decked paths led down to a stunning bay. In the holiday season it must have been a popular place, but on a weekday in October it was all for me. There was an entrance gate with a kiosk but, as often, the barrier was left open, because the sea is for all to enjoy and the sea should be free; unless the army has taken over, that is.

I had heard it hardly ever rains in Antalya but the forecast said it would, and it did. In preparation, I bought enough food and water and took cover in my tent at a lovely campsite, set between craggy hills, near the archeological site of Olympus. I bumped into a guy called Leo, who was a young Russian and a climber instructor. He told me how his life had been turned upside down; with a brother living in Ukraine and the rest of his relatives in Russia, he had been forced to flee his country to avoid fighting against his own family. Antalya has always been a popular destination for Russian tourists looking for a break and sunshine. What was different now, as he told me, was that about a million Russians had escaped to Turkey to avoid being conscripted into the army and sent to fight. He further told me how futile it was to protest in his country, as it landed you straight into jail. My heartfelt wish for him was that the war would soon be over so that he could rejoin his family; we said goodbye, both agreeing that peace and freedom were far better and should never be taken for granted. At nightfall the storm approached, announced by lightning and frightful thunder echoing around the valley. Then rain fell in buckets and strong gusts of wind tested the tents of this bunch of brave campers. In the morning it calmed down, leaving skewed and twisted clouds hanging in a dull grey sky. I spoke to the campsite owner about the stormy night; he admitted it had been pretty bad, so much so that he had jumped into his car and driven away to spend the night at home, hoping everything would be alright.

All that was left of my journey were two small hills and a flat stretch of coastline. With the weather still unsettled I thought I should linger and wait for a blue sky, but I gambled in order to get closer without having to rush against time. After the first hill was climbed and it was starting to drizzle, I stopped at a busy restaurant filled with locals. Its car park contained all the good omens; there were lots of cars parked but mostly, lots of lorries. I had some tender lamb stewed in onions, flat bread still hot from the oven and a fresh salad: the best meal I had had so far. I reached the city of Antalya on an overcast day. It had taken me three weeks and well over a thousand kilometres of cycling to get a little soaked for the first time. No wonder that cyclists often talk of Turkey as one of the highlight destinations. The country certainly did not disappoint me: sometimes modern and sometimes dilapidated, overbuilt and chaotic in its large cities while vast and peaceful in its countryside. The warmth and hospitality of its people is what will mostly stand out in my memory. People always happy to lend a hand, and make everything look easy when you thought it might be impossible or difficult. I hope in the future I will once more hear those *merhaba*, those sincere welcomes and thanks for being a customer, but mostly for having cycled and stopped in their otherwise unremarkable village. There is much more to this country. I have left Cappadocia, its mountains and its interiors, largely unexplored, hoping for another chance and for more Turkey to look forward to.

* * *

Colombian Andes

Colombian Andes

Long haul travel was finally back, after almost three years during which it had been too complicated, if not downright impossible. To celebrate my regained ability to roam freely, I thought I would return to South America, where I had narrowly escaped the start of the pandemic that had thrown a spanner into world travel. I chose Colombia as my next destination. The country was passionate about cycling, had decent roads and a year-round warm climate; it had also recently become relatively safe after decades of unrest, welcoming back travellers. When planning my route I thought it best to avoid the excessive humidity and heat of the coast and opted for a ride that would allow me to visit some of its best preserved old towns as well as take in some of the majestic scenery of the Andes.

After a night spent crossing the Atlantic, I took a domestic flight to the city of Bucaramanga in order to get close to San Gil where my ride would finally start. I breathed a sigh of relief as I assembled my bike: once again it had been well looked after during its long journey across the world. The small regional airport offered a great welcome to a travelling cyclist. Set on top of a mountain plateau, access to Bucaramanga was via a pleasant downhill ride that dived down fifteen kilometres before reaching the city centre. That was exactly what I needed after a long journey without enough rest. The friendly hotel owner did not mind me arriving far too early; she let me check-in and allowed me to get some welcome rest before taking a short walk to experience the smells, sights and sounds of a new country.

The following day I had to make one last short transfer; a three hour bus journey to San Gil. The start was slow due to a horrible traffic jam caused by a taxi drivers' strike that blocked city roads all over

Colombia. Once past the rows of stationery yellow taxis that were blocking all but one lane, we started moving, winding our way through the spectacular Chicamocha Canyon: two hundred kilometres long and up to 2,000 metres deep, it is often tipped as being the second-largest on the planet. I would have loved to cycle it, but it would have taken three more days, time that I did not have. I reached San Gil around lunchtime; it was advertised as the outdoor sports capital of the country and I was eager to get started with a short day of cycling. I once again assembled my bike and loaded my luggage under the curious stares of a bunch of youngsters. I had planned a relatively easy climb of a couple of hours; just enough to get me adjusted to the exercise, the road traffic and the high altitudes which would accompany me for most of the journey. It would bring me to the historic gem that is the village of Barichara. One of Colombia's best preserved colonial villages, it was founded in 1705 and retains lots of the original white clay buildings and streets paved with cobblestones that make it a favourite location for movie makers shooting dramas set in colonial times.

Barichara lived up to its reputation, and proved to be an ideal introduction to the rest of the country. After the warm welcome of Selina at El Principito, one of the many historic properties turned into guest houses, I wandered up and down its streets, thrown back to a long lost time. It was Ash Wednesday and the beginning of Lent. The streets that had been buzzing with people in the afternoon turned quiet as the whole village attended mass. I had dinner in the main square, not far from the cathedral, its doors left wide open in order to accommodate the overflowing crowds. Life re-emerged an hour later as people with smiling faces filled the square; they had all been forgiven for their sins with a black ash sign of the cross painted on their foreheads as a reminder.

The following morning I was sitting in the peaceful garden of the guest house waiting for breakfast; I told Selina how lucky she was to have been born and to live in such a special place.

- Barichara, COLOMBIA -

No wonder she always looked so jovial and happy. I mentioned it to her and agreed with the wisdom that was in her answer.

"Nothing good comes out of being miserable anyway..." she said.
"One might as well keep smiling."

The owner of the guest house, she told me, was a Frenchman who had visited the town on holiday for the first time a year earlier and had fallen in love with it so much that he had decided to return and make it his home. I also heard he had fallen for a Colombian girl, which must have surely played some part in it! Selina started talking about marriage and family; I felt it was coming and I was ready for it.

"You are alone here? Aren't you married?" She asked.

I struggled to articulate any meaningful thoughts in my toddler Spanish, but she must have got the gist of it as she looked utterly horrified.

"One needs a wife and family to be happy..." she told me.

The language barrier was too big to try to justify the life choices of those who, like myself, don't fit into a predestined mould and decide that there is life beyond family and marriage; I am sure even perfect eloquence would have failed. All I could do was to nod at what she was saying and be grateful for her sincere concerns.

"Well...," she ended politely " as long as one is happy..."

I could tell she did not believe any of it. She served me breakfast with a lukewarm smile, while her jolly mood turned a little sombre.

Before departing, as I was thanking her for her welcome and warmth, my grasp of Spanish once more failed me. She was sitting at a table with a young girl whom I had seen the day before - and had assumed must be her daughter, as they looked much alike.

"*Es tu hermana?*" I asked in my best pronunciation.

They burst out laughing as I realised that *hermana* actually meant sister and my Spanish had a long way to go to help me travel safely.

I reluctantly left the peace of Barichara and started cycling across the same green hills on this clear cloudless day. Along the road past San Gil I spotted a second hand car dealer and got the sudden urge to acquire a Colombian car registration plate that I obtained on this record breaking second day. Along the way I was introduced to the country's sense of humour: a signpost belonging to a restaurant advertised a menu of fruit salads, sandwiches, tropical fruit juices and divorces.

I reached Socorro in the early afternoon. The town holds a special place in Colombia's history. It is here that the revolution of the *Comuneros* started. This was the revolt against the country's Spanish rulers that eventually led to Simon Bolivar winning the fight for independence. I walked around the city centre, which was otherwise unremarkable, before it was time to check-in at the guest house. I got a little lost on the way and Adriana, my host, had almost given up waiting for me and was walking out of her front door to do some shopping. I had messaged her earlier, telling her I was cycling around the country, so when she spotted a foreigner looking lost and pushing a bicycle, she waved at me from a distance. She turned out to be a kind, original and somehow quirky person. Before sitting down to register me, she turned on her hi-fi system, tuning it to a channel broadcasting new age meditation tunes that almost put me to sleep. She was the local Reiki practitioner as well as holistic healer. She showed me around her back garden, where tidy rows of medicinal plants were growing in order to be used in her healing practice. She was a writer and used to paint too, she told me, before arthritis put an end to it and forced her to move to sculpture. I told her I did not know much about Reiki but mentioned my life long interest in Eastern spirituality and Buddhism.

"I knew it!" she said, all excited.
"Everybody that comes to stay here is drawn by a mysterious energy."

She wanted to take a picture with me, but only if I had a photo filter that could remove the wrinkles on her face. I didn't, and tried to suggest that she shouldn't worry too much about it.

"Well... you are a man," she said, "all women are like this."

We chatted a while and she started asking profound questions on the meaning of life that I would have struggled to answer in English let alone in Spanish. She asked whether I wanted to meditate with her in the garden; I told her I needed some rest after a day of cycling, unintentionally suggesting that meditation could be tiring. She insisted in showing me a tiny pond with a path around it:

"All the energy from the planets converges here..." she said.

I nodded. It was said with such firm conviction that I wondered whether she might know something that I didn't and that she might be right. Unfortunately there was nothing holistic or healing about my room's mattress; it was badly sagging and woke me up in the middle of the night with back pain.

I was jotting down notes in my diary and had planned on writing how Colombia's stray dogs had so far been harmless and well behaved. I thought it must be down to cycling popularity and them being used to seeing cyclists. I was wrong and never got a chance to write it. I had hardly left Socorro and was descending into a deep valley when four small dogs started chasing me and barking. I didn't think much about it, ignored them and kept pedalling until I felt the teeth of one of them sinking into my heel for the first time in my life. It didn't bite me too much. The farm owner who had failed to prevent the dogs from chasing me was very apologetic. A little shocked, I thought I should move on, but then noticed that what seemed at first a minor scratch was now trickling with blood. I stopped a few houses further up the hill where an elderly man was standing by his gate and asked for some alcohol to disinfect it. His name was Humberto and he spoke some English. He ran to the house and returned with some disinfectant that he sprayed generously on my ankle. As it happened he was a friend of the doctor in Oiba, the next village, that was about an hour away. He phoned him, to ensure that he would be waiting for this wounded cyclist. I reached the medical practice and was welcomed by his son at the entrance; he had been waiting for me and whisked me through the queue of patients and sat me down in a room, eager to practise some English while I had swirling thoughts about catching rabies. Doctor Moreno spoke only Spanish but sounded calm and reassuring. I was moved to a treatment room where a team of four was assembled; there was the doctor, his wife and a nurse taking care of the wound, while his son was doing the translating. An anti tetanus shot was advised. I was told it was something I would have normally had to get from a local hospital but a round of phone calls did it. Someone went off to the local hospital and returned after thirty minutes and the injection was given. The doctor suggested three days of complete rest and prescribed a course of antibiotics and analgesic pills to keep me busy for the rest of the week. Despite the accident I did not feel too bad and wanted to reach the place I had booked for my night's stay so I kept gently cycling. I arrived at Casa Redonda, which was right on top of a hill and reached after a steep walk that seemed to last a lifetime. Antonio and his wife were waiting for me and listened to my adventures, and they kindly invited me to join them for a simple dinner. Antonio was a retired sociology professor and cheered me up saying I should not be too worried about the dog's bite.

"A few years ago my wife was bitten twice on the same day..." he said, trying to reassure me.

The early morning views from the balcony of Casa Redonda were stunning. Low clouds enveloped the hills down below and all around it, while the sun rose over the high mountains. Antonio sat down for breakfast with me, complaining about the messy state of his country. In the nineties when Colombia was off-limits to tourists on grounds of safety, he said there were a total of six armies. There was the official government's army and five private ones, just as big, financed by profits from narco traffic. Each fought a constant war in an effort to keep control of their territories and road access, as well as keeping people on their side.

"Now there are seven," he said, "but the new leftist government has changed tactics."

Apparently a deal was struck between them and the government. The rogue armies agreed to less violence while the latter promised to close both eyes whenever necessary. He showed me for the first time what a coffee plant and raw coffee beans look like. As far as my heel went, I felt no pain and there was no swelling which seemed promising. Still he insisted on driving me down to the village pharmacist to get the wound cleaned and checked one more time. Once there, a young and cheerful pharmacist, who had an excellent grasp of the English language, dressed and cleaned the wound and filled me with hope and positivity. I was relieved to hear that so far everything looked fine and that she thought nothing serious would come out of it. She said to not bother keeping a gauze bandage over it or using the cream and disinfectant that the doctor had sold me, and she further cheered me up by telling me there was no reason to stop cycling. She asked to see the antibiotics I had been given and burst out laughing when she realised they were the wrong type. These ones were for the urinary system. Despite this, as I had started taking them, she said I should continue.

"They won't do any harm to your leg," she joked "and you will have a brand new bladder by the end of it."

The mist and low clouds of the early morning lifted, as did the weight from my shoulders. The night before I had been browsing the internet, reading reports about rabies. I read pages upon pages of bad news that if anything succeeded in getting me extremely worried. There seemed to be a consensus that if one had the bad luck to get it, only certain death puts an end to the excruciating pain! I thanked Antonio and the pharmacist and moved on, continuing cycling towards Boyaca, a region that has produced most of Colombia's professional cyclists. I spent a night at a coffee farm above the town of Barbosa where Crispino, his wife Gladys and son Camillo introduced me to all the varieties of plants they were growing. The green fruit, as it matures, turns red and is then ready to be picked, while the thin sweet outer peel can also be eaten as it is. Scattered in their garden were large wooden frames with metal grids where the kernels were left to dry under the sun for up to four days. Next was the storage room where large bags had been filled with raw beans, ready to be shipped all over the planet. Camillo, who had studied law at a Bogotà university, spoke excellent English. He translated what his dad was telling me but was also himself very knowledgeable about the coffee business. Initially, as he told me, he had not been much interested in his dad's trade, but after graduating he began to appreciate his luck in having a good income and a future served up on his plate and decided to learn the intricacies of coffee growing.

"There are far too many lawyers in Colombia anyway…" he told me.

"Most of them are really bad, but with so much competition the pay is not as good as one would think".

I was curious as to why in a country that produces some of the best coffee beans in the world, what I had been served so far at most cafés was a bland brew that lacked aroma and flavour. Camillo told me that all good coffee produced in Colombia goes elsewhere.

"Most Colombians don't even have a chance to try it." he said.
"What you get in most places is the bad quality stuff that nobody else wants, and when that runs out, the leftovers from Peru, Ecuador or some other South American country."

Another issue was the lack of good machines and expertise in roasting. Apparently only a few of these were available in Bogotà, but they were still no match for those found in Europe's coffee loving countries. Of course, producing the stuff, the Tua family was an exception and Camillo was keen to have me try some really nice coffee, as strong as an Italian thinks it should be. Amongst the courses he had attended to improve his knowledge and skills, Camillo had also trained as a coffee taster. He poured a freshly brewed cup and followed it with a demonstration and lengthy instructions:
"First suck the coffee up to get some air in." he told me as I sipped the beverage with a slurp that pleased him.

"Next, swirl it around the mouth and put some on the top of the tongue for two seconds before swallowing it."

"That way you will get a sweet aftertaste and appreciate the flavour fully."

He was so passionate about the subject that, in order not to disappoint him, I pretended to get it; in reality I failed to notice any difference from simply drinking a cup without making a scene. There was too much technique and too many expectations, and I thought the sounds and mouth contortions involved in it were not something that should be practised at a busy café.

Barbosa was buzzing with shoppers and youngsters ready to be merry on a Saturday night of partying. I joined them for a short while, wandering the streets in search of food and some strong sunscreen. Once back at the *finca cafetera* all was quiet. Gladys introduced me to the local game of *ranas*, frogs. A wooden cabinet with holes in it and a few nailed-in metal frogs with open mouths was set at the end of the passageway. Thin metal disks were thrown from a distance, aiming for the frogs' mouth or the holes that awarded most points. Since she was retired and had plenty of time on her hands, she was a master at it and obviously trashed me. She also had a creative way of keeping the tally, always adding a bit to hers while shaving off some from mine. Once Crispino returned home from the fields he joined us, switching on one of those 'smart' speakers one talks to; he pestered the patient gadget with request after request of popular Latin tunes that often produced the wrong results leaving him a little frustrated and disappointed with technology. They both talked a lot, telling me things in Spanish as if I was a native. It often happened in Colombia; people felt I was fluent in the language while in reality I was at best making guesses in Italian, another latin language, but otherwise listened and nodded politely. Whether Crispino's song request had been granted or not, the two of them eventually started dancing before we all said good night.

I next headed to the historic town of Villa de Leyva, pleased that despite the anti tetanus shot and all the antibiotics the legs were still turning nicely. It was rather the lungs that were struggling; it took about three hours of climbing to reach the mountain pass at an altitude of 2500 metres in the village of Santa Sofia. From then on, tired but satisfied, I knew it would be all downhill. I did not descend much though as Villa de Leyva sits on a plain well above two thousand metres. The town was the busiest so far in Colombia. A three hour bus journey from Bogotá, it is a tourist hub and one of the highlights of a visit to Colombia. As was the case with Barichara, the historic centre was criss-crossed by a regular grid of cobbled streets, retaining the look from centuries past.

- Villa de Leyva, COLOMBIA -

Tourism of course had brought a host of guest houses, restaurants, travel agents and shops, but everything was most tastefully done and in harmony. I strolled around the town at my favourite time of day, when the sun is about to set or about to rise; only then can one experience places in the best light. Villa de Leyva surely had an idyllic setting, spreading on a flat plateau surrounded by the green tall slopes of the Andes, and it had a bearable temperature even at the height of summer.

Because of time constraints I took a bus transfer from Villa de Leyva to the capital Bogotá where I rested a couple of days while enjoying some city sightseeing. Ten million people living at such a high altitude can't be any good. Colombia, I was told, was now much safer, yet crime was still an issue in larger cities like this. The general advice given to foreigners staying in La Candelaria, which is the city centre, was to enjoy it by day while being extremely cautious if wandering out at night. Bogotá compensates for its lack of spectacular landmarks with a vibrant life, the constant background beats of Latin sounds and an incredible display of graffiti. In the historic quarter of La Candelaria a house or a simple wall often turns into the perfect canvas on which young folk with talent produce the most colourful works of art. I took the cable car to the top of Monserrate, where a Christ statue and a sanctuary are perched right on top of the mountain, granting incredible views over the vastness of the city. Next there were lots of gold artefacts at *Museo de Oro*, allegedly the best in the whole continent. The rest of my time was spent wandering the worn out alleys of the city centre, with their thrilling hustle and bustle of life and their kaleidoscope of colourful graffitis.

There was the regular reminder to keep alert. Policemen stood around busy corners and junctions with massive Rottweilers on the leash; they certainly looked ready for action whenever help was needed. They also reminded me that, despite the misfortune, I had been lucky to have been bitten by a poodle.

- Bogotà, COLOMBIA -

The main part of the journey was about to start; I had planned a route from Bogotá to Medellin, ten challenging days of cycling up and down the central range of the Andes or *Cordillera Central* as it is known in Spanish. The highest climb along the way, and the biggest hurdle of them all, was going to be Alto de Letras, at an altitude of 3700 metres. I had done a decent job in planning this adventure, starting off with a few gentle days training on the hills of Boyaca followed by a couple of rest days at high altitude. Now ready to tackle more serious mountains, it was time to leave Bogotá well rested and acclimatised. At the start I had to navigate through the whole length of the city and was prepared to battle against some bad traffic. It turned out to be easy. A lesser known fact about Bogotá is that it happens to be the cycling capital of South America. Over the years a remarkable cycle route network had been built, making it easy to cross what would otherwise be an intimidating metropolis. I was told by locals to start cycling later in the morning, just after the early commuter traffic, and that also turned out to be good advice. By nine o'clock most traffic was coming from the opposite side towards the city centre and for the most part I could enjoy riding along excellent cycleways that could have competed in quality with the best Dutch ones. Even better than in Holland was the fact that along Bogotá's cycleways there were plenty of wandering mechanics waiting; their spare parts and tools were arranged on a blanket by the side and they were ready to fix most emergencies and to make ends meet.

The worst of the traffic was met once outside the city, where the cycleways stopped and a road turned into a highway. Lorries and buses were competing for the faster lanes while I made slow progress in the emergency lane by the side. The majority of trucks found in Colombia are humongous American trucks well past their prime-time. Their large exhaust pipes spewed pitch black diesel fumes into the sky or right into my face as they passed by. Certainly not great for the lungs but, as far as the heel went, I had completed the week's course of antibiotics and was grateful it had healed well and that I felt fine. Beyond the city I had it easy; I continued on flat roads helped by tailwinds until the town of Facatativà. What followed was a steep descent from Bogotá's high plateau to a green, tropical forest valley. I lost over a thousand metres of altitude, something that I would surely have to regain over the next few days.

I spent the night at yet another coffee farm. Mario and his wife lived in a simple one storey building to the side, while I was the only tourist in a dark, three storey brick house that stuck out like a sore thumb in the tropical landscape. At breakfast I was asked whether I wanted some juice. Mario walked briskly down to the garden with a long pole and picked a couple of oranges from one of his trees; he returned after a few minutes squeezing the freshest juice one could possibly get. I felt in good shape for the tough ride that awaited me, a long stage that involved climbing a couple of mountains. The humidity at that lower altitude was brutal and were it not for the nice Merino wool I was wearing I would have drowned in my own sweat. Thankfully, Colombian engineers seemed to have grasped the art of constructing roads to perfection. They dealt with the challenges posed by rough and steep mountains in the most elegant of manners, with twists and turns that climbed gently around them. As for the dogs, they were still chasing me. I experienced three attempted attacks in a day but by now I knew better; I religiously stopped each time and they always lost any interest in me and walked away bored and confused. I stopped at a roadside café to get a cold drink. A lorry driver was fascinated by the small parked bicycle. He inspected it carefully, paying attention to how I had loaded my luggage; he then looked at me smiling, wondering aloud whether one day he should do the same and make it to the border of the United States in search of a better life. This was a common refrain I would hear from time to time, the struggle and strife of living in a wonderful country where decades of crime and corruption made it a hard place to stay.

After having topped the first mountain, I descended to the humidity and dampness of the lovely village of Guadas; not as picture perfect, but it reminded me of Barichara. While cycling out of town I met Nelson who coasted along with me on a mountain bike for a while. He wore an elegant black suit and a spotless white shirt, and was the elementary school maths teacher and a keen cyclist. He asked whether I could wait for him to get changed so that he could join me on the way up the second mountain. I thought I should keep going but told him that, with all the luggage, I was not a fast rider and he would probably be able to catch up with me. I was slow, but never saw him again. Once I had conquered the last obstacle of the day I could enjoy a long descent and after crossing the Navarro bridge over the river Magdalena, allegedly the first iron bridge ever built in South America, I entered the town of Honda. Set in a valley well below one thousand metres, it had the climate of a steam oven. It seemed I was not the only one to suffer and complain about it as there was a lot of huffing and puffing as well as handkerchiefs wiping sweat drops from foreheads. My bedroom at the guest house had a giant ceiling fan that I had to leave running all night, trusting it would not fall apart and decapitate me. Despite the slight wobble as it spun around, it held in place.

Monica and her mom prepared a hearty breakfast to set me off on a good start. After a few glimpses of the Cordillera Oriental at the start of the journey, the *Rio Magdalena* marked the border of the Cordillera Central, the central part of the Andes that I would have to deal with all the way to Medellin. The start of the new day was flat and the weather overcast. The flat landscape of grassy fields and palm trees reminded me of past trips in Thailand and Sri Lanka. Once I reached Mariquita the comfort of flat roads left me as I started climbing the first kilometres of Alto de Letras. I would have to gain more than three thousand metres in altitude to get there, something that would keep me busy for at least two days. I began the first few ramps knowing that I was cycling in the tropics. Any effort in such places involves lots of sweating and a lingering smell that follows one. First you wonder whether it might be a tree, an exotic fruit or a flower, or possibly some kind of animal decomposing. Eventually it dawns on you that humidity and heat soak clothes and that everything turns mouldy. I moved in and out of intricate forests where each tree competed for any available inch of light. Thankfully, along the road was an endless series of improvised stalls that were a blessing for the dehydrated cyclists; often at the side of ramshackle houses and huts they had a small fridge with cool drinks on sale. I ended the day in Fresno, the last sizeable town where one can get food and accommodation.

The night turned stormy with a threatening display of lightning and it was still raining when I woke up early in the morning. I checked out but sat on a sofa in the lobby hoping for a quick miracle and some sun to arrive. After one hour it was still drizzling but the sky had turned lighter and, thinking it was as good as it would get, I left anyway. As I moved higher up the mountain the clouds scattered and I could even enjoy a brief ride in the sunshine. I was struggling and panting up a steep hill when a couple of teenagers on rickety bikes sped past me showing me how it really should be done. Each held a rope with a metal hook tied to a lorry's rear bumper and they overtook me with grins of enjoyment for the effortless ride. I had planned a short day, only a few hours of climbing to reach the last hotel available before tackling the remaining kilometres to reach the top of the climb. For the first time I regretted not having a tent with me as I would have been able to go a little further, making it easier on the following day. I had forty kilometres left to climb instead, before the long descent into Manizales. I reached Padua on a busy Saturday, the only *'gringo'* in a quiet mountain village that had suddenly come to life. A thick fog descended, enveloping the mountains all around, as hifi speakers started competing with each other by increasing their volumes; the main street was transformed into an open-air party; another week was over and it was time to be merry and mesmerised by the thumping rhythms and sounds of Cumbia and Reggeaton.

    I set a six o'clock alarm call. I had to leave early if I was ever going to make it. A quick glance outside the window didn't leave much hope. The fog was still there, so thick that from the second floor I could hardly see the trees in the back garden. In the time it took to get my luggage ready nothing short of a miracle happened. I checked out and opened the hotel front door and realised that in hardly thirty minutes it had all changed and it was now all clear and sunny. I stopped by the same coffee place I had visited the previous night and ordered two slices of the same tasty orange cake. I started cycling up the mountain, taking in some spectacular views down the valley. I started the slow countdown to the top feeling blessed to have been granted such a promising day. I stopped frequently at rickety stalls, replenishing energy with fried eggs, bananas, flat cornbread and bowls of *agua de panela*, a traditional sweet drink made with sugarcane. It has a peculiar flavour and I was told that Colombian professional cyclists never leave the country without it. After six hours I reached the top, joining up for ritual pictures with a bunch of road cyclists who had sped past me with their light carbon fibre bikes. After a quick meal there was no time to waste and I was keen to descend to Manizales. On the other side of the mountain I faced a completely different climate. The fog that had vanished in the morning reappeared, giving an eerie veil to the landscape. For the first time in my life I felt cold in a tropical climate. I descended wrapped in all the clothes I carried, disappearing in a grey soup pierced only by the headlights of cars and trucks approaching. Manizales came with a surprise. I hadn't done any research and what I thought would be a large mountain town turned out to be a city with half a million inhabitants and a traffic system that was hell for cyclists. A heavy downpour followed me all the way to the city centre and I reached the hotel soaked to the bones and dripping but happy to have made it alive. I am sure Manizales on a clear day must have been a nice place to visit. Built on a series of steep hills, its main public transport consisted of a series of cable cars linking them. Streets were a rundown version of downtown San Francisco, climbing up impossible gradients before diving down steeply on the other side. I spent the evening strolling along central *Carrera 23* and visited its imposing neo gothic cathedral. I didn't get to see enough of Manizales; it remained covered in mist and fog until the following morning when it was already time to leave.

    I was deep in the Zona Cafetera, the main coffee producing area in the country thanks to its ideal climate. Sturdy plants with thick, dark leaves and green and red fruits clung everywhere along the steep banks of the road to Neira. This route had been suggested by an acquaintance; it twisted up and down lush mountains, at times offering exceptional views and blissfully devoid of traffic. Colombia is blessed by an unrivalled variety of flora and fauna and I cycled on an ever present soundtrack of the most unfamiliar sounds. I arrived in beautiful Salamina with its idyllic setting and colourful alleys just before sunset. There was still life in the streets with busy shops catering for a small crowd of locals as well as tourists.

- Salamina, COLOMBIA -

A new day began with a thrilling descent, an easy start to new challenges. This area of Colombia doesn't do flats.
Its topography is rugged like the faces of those *campesinos* I saw gathering in the main town square in the early morning, patiently pleading for farming work and drawing attention with a raised arm. Each descent was immediately followed by another climb and in no time I was back to the grindstone, at times wishing I had chosen the Caribbean coast and its sandy beaches instead. The humidity made it more tiring, and I had to remind myself that some discomfort was a price worth paying in order to fully appreciate such a fascinating landscape. In a few hours I was back down to eight hundred metres one more time before having to climb up the two thousand metres of

altitude at Las Coles. I must have walked a good third of it! Farmers tended coffee plants, sugar cane and plantains and seemed surprised to see a foreigner on a messy road that was obviously ill suited to cycling. They had long *machetes* dangling from their belts but were, thankfully, extremely friendly. Colombia does take care of and loves its cyclists. There were whistles coming from motorbikes and jeeps speeding past me, which I assumed were more for the stoic effort than the looks. There were also cries of *'guapo'* which, according to my dictionary, meant handsome. but they mostly came from elderly men and did not flatter me. Dark clouds gathered around me as I was about to start yet another climb. A few kilometres from Aguadas, there was a rumble of thunder and the heavens opened. I sat on a wooden bench covered by four square metres of asbestos, which was a godsend in a tropical downpour. Had I been in the 'developed world', I would have been hopelessly stuck halfway up the mountain, but not in Colombia. In such places, discomfort and inconvenience bring simple yet impeccable solutions. Who needs bus stops and timetables? Buses arrive when they do, which still seems more often in the Andes than in peak time central London. A simple wave of a hand and they pick you up there and then and a *'puedes tomar aqui'* or some other basic Spanish, works wonders to ask them to let you get off wherever you want to.

    I had been waiting before giving a final verdict but I would say that Colombia is going through a bit of a gastronomic ice age. Not unlike how the British suffered in the last century, before being rescued by a barrage of television cookery programs and an influx of talented chefs from Europe, India and China. It is a fact that you are unlikely to find many Colombian restaurants outside the country. I don't want to seem unkind. Maybe like coffee, the best food the country produces is exported or reserved only for the top restaurants and they have to make do with what is left. Happy looking cows grazed on luxurious pastures, yet those few times I ordered a steak by the end of the meal my jaw hurt from the lengthy munching. After a few days I decided I should stick to staples such as roast chicken, beans and hamburgers. Lack of tasty food is offset by an incredible variety of delicious fruits. Besides the familiar oranges, bananas, mandarins, pineapple, mango and papaya there were plenty more I had never seen or even heard of. There were *mangosteen, goldenberry, gulupa, dragon fruit, granadilla, lula, guanabana, chontaduro, maracuyá, zapote, birojó, nispero*...and the list went on and on. Maybe to compensate for the sometimes bland taste of food they used them in the most peculiar ways. I was once served chicken soup with a plantain on the side. I looked around to see what other customers were doing with it. A chap was dunking it in and seemed perfectly happy with it. Another time I was surprised to discover that orange slices had found their way into my beef stew. At a gourmet burger place in the town of Honda they presented a perfectly decent burger and fries with a watermelon slice pinned on top with a toothpick.

I left a chilly Aguadas as the mountains around me played hide and seek, wrapping around low clouds and blurred by the unmissable fog of the Andes. Cows and sheep grazed unfazed as if in a balancing act, feasting on grass on precipitous pastures. I had my daily dose of dog encounters: most of them ended fine while some verged on the nasty and necessitated a stop and some shouting. I had by now perfected the art of getting off a moving bike as soon as I heard some barking and felt that a chase was about to happen. I dropped all the way down to the banks of the river Arma and the Rio Cauca, following a rough road through a steamy forest with the deafening sounds of birds and insects. Mountains disappeared and the narrow valleys opened up at La Pintada. There was only one more mountain range between me and the end of another journey. From there it was all the way up to the village of Santa Barbara de Antioquia.

The road had recently suffered a huge landslide, blocking all car traffic. However, I was told I would be fine on a bicycle and could enjoy what would have otherwise been a busy road to Medellin, accompanied by just a few motorbikers and a handful of cyclists. The final day dawned, with a last push to top Alto de Minas, a pass reaching 2440 metres of altitude, before dropping down into Pablo Escobar's infamous city. Legs were aching and the weather was still misty. For a brief moment, from the vantage point of the guest house rooftop terrace, I could glimpse through a break in the thick layer of clouds, for a last grand view and a farewell to the Andes. I made it to the top dry, but as soon as the descent started the rain pelted down and I was forced to take cover in a restaurant. After a time it lightened up and I could continue downhill until I reached the outskirts of Medellin and its built up traffic; my host in Santa Barbara had suggested I should take a taxi to reach the city centre as it was much safer. Just as I was about to call it quits after several dangerous close calls with trucks and yellow taxis, I spotted a cycle route that took me safely much further. I knew for sure that it would not be easy to find my guest house and felt I had already tempted fate enough. Outside a shopping mall, not too far from the city centre, there was a long queue of Korean made taxis with a dispatcher organising them. I stopped and asked for a lift to Candelaria. She looked at me a little puzzled:

"And what about the bike, darling...?"

My Spanish was not up to the task of explaining the intricacies of a bike folding mechanism that would fit into the tiniest of Hyundai, and I was too tired to even try. I performed the well rehearsed miracle of folding metal and made everything disappear inside a large plastic bag surrounded by the enthusiastic comments of the drivers.

"Que guapo!"

      I had arrived in a city that a couple of decades earlier was the most dangerous place on earth with ridiculously high murder rates. It still felt a somewhat complicated place, as had been Bogotá, but according to locals it had experienced a complete turnaround and an unlikely revival. Tourists had slowly returned and were walking around, still a little wary and mindful that even today a wrong turn could land you in a lot of trouble.

Reminders of worse times were still to be seen in a city where most entrance doors were protected by metal gates and bars were fitted on windows, screaming of crime and mistrust. A far cry from what I had experienced cycling in the countryside, up and down Colombia's mountains and through colourful villages that had filled with joyfulness and kindness.

Across Hokkaido

Across Hokkaido

Twenty years have passed since I first cycled in Japan, a place I have become rather familiar with and which, despite its peculiar customs and culture, feels like home from home. The Japan I have become accustomed to is that of Tokyo and Honshu island, where an endless sprawl of cities merges seamlessly, making the most of every inch of flatland, often ending up in a mess of concrete and electrical cables. That side of the country has its own fascination but, as far as cycling goes, I had always wanted to visit Hokkaido, not as busy and inhabited, where space is plenty and nature still holds its place. After far too many hours spent on a plane, and horrendously jet-lagged, I made it to Chitose International Airport on the outskirts of Sapporo, its main city. Under a late summer sun I found a quiet corner and set myself the usual first task of assembling the bicycle and getting started. I filled a large black bin bag with layers of cardboard and other packaging and, in a spotless and sanitised terminal, began wondering what could be done about it.

How to dispose of rubbish is a common problem faced by foreigners visiting the country. Whether it is the truth or a myth, it is said that after the 1995 Tokyo subway Sarin attack, which killed thirteen people, severely injured fifty more and temporarily damaged the eyesight of thousands, authorities took the drastic decision to remove the rubbish bins from roads, stations and all public places. In a country that's world famous for convenience, efficiency and all kinds of practicalities, this problem sticks out like a sore thumb. If you are a resident, you can always fill your pockets and dispose of it all once you are back in your apartment, but for everyone else it is hopeless and one has to become very creative. I didn't want to resort to fly tipping, further denting the bad reputation of foreigners, with their supposed lack of respect for etiquette and manners. I walked inside the terminal with my black rubbish bag and asked the first security officer I could find in the domestic terminal. He looked at me and, shaking his head, started hissing by breathing in through tightly pursed lips, a very Japanese way of diffusing the panic if unable to provide an answer. He aimlessly led me around in circles before stopping and bowing to me, admitting that we were searching for something that simply did not exist. He next gestured to follow him to a ticket desk where an airline employee was getting ready for a busy check in. She was also at a loss; she made a phone call to find an answer, or politely pretended to, before shaking her head, admitting that a few rubbish bins here and there would in fact prove quite useful.

The security officer's law-abiding nature started to crumble and he told me that given the situation I could discreetly dump the rubbish bag in a hidden corner by the cleaning staff office as someone would eventually deal with it. He smiled and waved goodbye before saying *ki o tsukete*, a phrase one hears often in Japan whose meaning is a little lost in translation but close to something like 'please be careful' or 'take good care of yourself'. I later wondered if he had known something I didn't because as soon as I got on the bike ready to leave, the bicycle chain snapped open and I lost my footing. It was the just reward for my own complacency. Months earlier, back from a trip to Colombia, I had opened the chain links to wash it and had then reassembled it. Testing the bike briefly before the trip, the chain had held in place and I had assumed all would be well, ignoring the inexorable law that says that if something can possibly go wrong, it will. I managed to temporarily fix it in order to at least reach the nearby town of Chitose where I had booked a night at a hostel.

After visiting a few bike shops unsuccessfully, I eventually found a mechanic willing to fit a new chain. What I thought would have been a straightforward job turned out to be tricky; the mechanic, like myself, didn't seem to be aware that chains come in different widths.

He first fitted a chain that was obviously too wide to work, before selecting a new one that would have been perfect had he not somehow managed to fit it the wrong way around the frame. Determined not to mess up more new chains, in a job that by now he regretted having accepted, he managed to fit the third one successfully. Feeling a little sorry for him, I bought some lubricant oil too, as a way of expressing my appreciation for his help, and all the time and good chains he had wasted! He said thank you, and was surely happy to see the back of me.

In the evening at the hostel I met mister Takigawa who had been sent to Hokkaido for a short business trip by his company. His knowledge of English was non-existent, and my Japanese was left wanting, but with a little help from his electronic dictionary he managed to tell me that his task was to test different types of concrete compounds, so many that it had taken him three days to complete. By the time I met him he had finished the work and was so bored with concrete that he was contemplating a career change. He asked how long my holiday was and was surprised when I told him it was just over two weeks; he gasped when I mentioned that I can usually take a couple of three week breaks each year. People are chronically overworked in Japan and for those wanting to climb the ladder in their companies even a single week consecutive holiday per year is hard to achieve. The following day being a Saturday, he was making the most of his company-sponsored journey to enjoy half a day of hiking before heading to the airport for the return flight. Mister Takigawa was curious about my travels on a bicycle and asked what had been the most dangerous country. I replied that it is often those with a bad reputation in the press that turn out to be the most welcoming. I mentioned the unreal kindness of Pakistani people as an example, telling him how hard it had been to pay for my own meals in a restaurant before someone else paid for me. After all the talking about generosity he asked whether I would like to join him for dinner, as he wanted to treat me. He was looking forward to his hike, he told me, although a little wary of bears. It is a well known fact that a hefty population of brown bears is thriving in Hokkaido and I had also come equipped with a little bell. In fact this turned out to be more of a talisman than something useful; it was meant to work with the swaying of the walker but was dead silent when hanging from the front of my cycle bag.

Japanese authorities take Health and Safety very seriously and aim to provide a life devoid of any danger. No wonder fear of bears was a common refrain in Hokkaido. During my first day of cycling I stopped a few times at rest places up in the mountains and noticed how tourists parked their cars and scanned the area with care before venturing out to reach the restrooms. I briefly chatted with a family from Tokyo:

"Aren't you scared to sleep in a tent?" The wife asked me.
"...and what would you do if you were chased by one while cycling?"

I mentioned my main worry was running out of water and, as they had been travelling by car from the opposite side, asked whether there was a place nearby where I could get some. The husband told me there was nowhere to get food or water until the next village about forty kilometres away, on the other side of the mountain. He kindly mentioned they might have some spare bottles of water in the car but returned a couple of minutes later holding two pots of drinking yoghurt instead. That is all he could find and he offered it to me, ignoring the disapproving looks of the children. I thanked him, and thanked the kids for their sacrifice, before waving goodbye as we headed our opposite ways. The forests were thick and the roads turned quiet, and her innocent questions about bears sprang to mind. I started feeling afraid. She was right after all. There really wasn't much I could do but pray that if I did encounter one along the road, it would at least happen on a steep downhill stretch. Otherwise I worried that my chances of survival could be slim!

- Takinoue, JAPAN -

The next day, Sunday morning, it felt as if half the population of Japan fancied a drive along route 274 in Hokkaido. Luck dictated that most of the traffic was in the opposite lane, but it was still annoying and relentless. At the same time, while climbing up and down the low mountains, a series of tunnels emerged. This is something I had experienced many years before when touring around the Alps on the main island. Tunnels are both a blessing and a curse for the cyclist. On the positive side there are two main advantages. First, nothing is as good as a tunnel to cut through the steepest parts of a mountain. Most cyclists, while not openly admitting it, dislike steep climbs and applaud every kilometre saved by such tunnels. Secondly, less effort improves the mood and lowers the blood pressure: no longer does the whole world seem to be against you. However, there are also negatives: what is good for the arteries is not so good for the lungs, inhaling the cars' exhaust fumes.

I thought the worst was over when I made it to the exit of Inasato tunnel, after twenty long minutes of walking along its emergency pavement. Hardly half a metre wide, it was too narrow to cycle along without risking falling over the side, committing a *harakiri* on tarmac in a spooky blackness lit only by cars' headlights. I was wrong. Hardly ten kilometres further on I entered the darkness of Hidaka Tunnel with a whopping length of two kilometres. I felt the right time had come to put on my reflecting, fluorescent, yellow vest, and reluctantly disappeared inside it. I had to endure another half an hour of bike pushing, while drivers flashed their full beam headlights, trying to figure out what the heck that bright yellow light was shining in the tunnel. I re-emerged, having acquired another layer of grime, thoroughly convinced that the inhaled fumes must have put an end to any viruses and germs still lurking in my body. Health and Safety in Japan had for the first time been found wanting. I believe foreigners intending to cycle in this country, upon first arrival, should undergo some sort of tunnel training, a tunnel-survival crash course that includes a signed waiver form for when things go pear shaped. I did survive, however, and crossed paths with a road cyclist on a light carbon fibre racing bike, about to play this Russian roulette from the opposite direction. It made me wonder about the average lifespan of a Japanese cyclist.

I reached the camping site in the ski resort of Hidaka. It was clearly not high season and there were only a few tents pitched on its vast grounds, mostly belonging to motorcyclists. They hardly charged anything for a pitch, and the setting and scenery was glorious. When I asked where the showers were, the receptionist pointed across the road, telling me that for a few more coins I could access the local bath spa or *onsen* as it is called in Japanese. These are great institutions that over the years I have grown to be very fond of; they fit perfectly into the Japanese way of life and culture and are the ultimate blessing for the travelling cyclist. I pitched my tent and headed straight there, keen to wash away the grime of those tunnels before enjoying a long and relaxing soak that restored my faith in the joys of this country.

With the weekend over, what had been busy roads turned quiet and devoid of much traffic. A man at the tourist information office told me that the summer season was officially over, which pleased me immensely. Japanese love to celebrate the arrival and change of seasons and, because of this, there is a season for pretty much everything. To the natural cycles of spring and its cherry blossom, or autumn when maple leaves change their colours, they add others which are more arbitrary. There is a season for climbing mountains, for example, which to us Europeans sounds rather bizarre. So Mount Fuji, for example, can be 'legally' climbed from beginning July to the beginning of September. Climbing it outside the official season is prohibited and likely means you are either a Japanese renegade or a foreigner unaware of the rules.

The hordes of tourists who had come to Hokkaido to get respite from the intolerable heat and humidity of summer on the main island had vanished, turning most roads into perfect cycling routes. The forecast spoke of a dull and cloudy day with a chance of some rain. I reached lake Kanayama on a grey and misty afternoon but an early morning sunrise broke through the clouds on the following day and the lake finally showed its face. Off-season Hokkaido had an end of the world feel that reminded me of outposts I had seen in Canada or in Patagonia. I crossed some ghostly little settlements with abandoned rickety buildings made of asbestos and tins. Its towns were mostly made out of prefabricated houses which if not exactly pretty seemed practical. One should not come expecting attractive or historic cities. The main reasons to visit Hokkaido are its national parks with their unspoilt nature, the chance to taste some excellent food and opportunities to soak in the hot spas, as well as get some excellent skiing in winter. I left Kanayama on the main road that follows the lake tightly before diverting and climbing through an expanse of forests with a series of long straights that gave plenty of opportunities to question the meaning of life. This tedious pedalling without the goal of an horizon was made more interesting by daydreams about what I would be eating once I reached Obihiro, the next big city. It was just a pleasing distraction that shifted between Ramen noodles, fried Tempura and sushi, never reaching any conclusion. A stream of large military vehicles started to trickle down the mountain, an unusual sight in a peace loving country. I wondered if Putin had gone completely berserk and, faced by an Ukrainian war that seemed to be going nowhere, had decided to surprise Japan from an island nearby.

Obihiro turned out to be a larger city than I had expected. If not much to write home about, it was a good place to find a hotel room and take cover from an afternoon drizzle that had been forecasted and arrived punctually. There, I realised what all that military kerfuffle was about; the city hosts the headquarters of the Fifth Division of the Japan Ground Self Defence Army. On a more useful note for cyclists, the city also takes pride in its excellent cuisine and is renowned for offering some of the best pork in the world. It lived up to its promise and simple marinated barbecued pork over a bowl of rice was one of the tastiest dishes I have ever had. I found the place by chance as I was looking for some dinner in the evening. I spotted an unassuming little corner shop near the station which would not have stood out were it not for the dozen people that were queuing patiently for a table. I also trusted the fact that the chef and single waiter were wearing a t-shirt with the writing 'since 1935'. I thought no restaurant could last that long in Japan, serving bland meals.

The sun shone again next morning. I left Obihiro and its square blocks and endless traffic lights to continue my ride in the Tokachi prefecture. Japanese towns and cities, not unlike the *imams* in Muslim countries, take pride in their speaker systems. Each town comes up with a particular song or jingle that is quiet for a few hours at night but otherwise plays on a loop that never fails to get under my skin. These jingle repetitions slowly but surely find a way into the brain not unlike song hooks; before you know it and regardless of how much you hate them, you soon find yourself humming along or whistling them. Speakers also have their usefulness. They trigger alarms in case of real or perceived emergencies, tell you whether you should carry an umbrella, wear sunscreen lotion or a hat to protect from sunstroke, and inform you that it has just struck midday; they never fail to warn and recommend you to be careful about something, and suggest reputable funeral services before trying to sell you an insurance policy. I suppose if you are born in a town you form a bond with its particular jingle. It must either make you lose the will to live or, if you move away for a while, get you very emotional once returning home, able to hear it again. Personally, they would quickly drive me insane or make me embark on an endless search from town to town until I found one with a tune I could put up with.

    In a culture with deep roots linked to Shintoism, and steeped in the contemplation of the arts and Zen Buddhism, one would imagine that silence is a treasure to be protected and nurtured. Surprisingly, Japanese cities and large towns make it hard to find respite from a constant bombardment of sounds. However, despite its quirks, I love Japan and its alien uniqueness that sets it apart from anywhere else on the planet. Having fondly bashed it for its excessive rules and regulations, it must be admitted that they also create a very secure society. Nowhere else in the world would I have felt safe leaving my Brompton bike unlocked for a long time or my luggage unattended. In most European cities, it would most likely disappear within ten minutes. In Obihiro, while spending an hour in a hot spa, I felt perfectly comfortable leaving it unlocked by the entrance, knowing that nobody would dare to even touch it. This removes a lot of the hassle that arises from carrying everything on our bikes while travelling.

In the town of Ikeda I met a young man with a camera and a massive telescopic zoom that must have cost twice as much as my bike. He was taking pictures by the entrance of a most uninteresting-looking building. I was curious and asked him about it. He had set himself the challenge of photographing as many post offices as he could find in the country! I wished him well and told him *ki o tsukete*, unaware of the risks involved in such a hobby. It probably also involved a fair bit of solitude, like my cycling. Whether my words of caution were appropriate or not he seemed to appreciate them and sincerely smiled back at me. I reached Honbetsu and its amazing free campsite with spotless toilets and coin-operated showers that lasted ten full minutes. For the following day the forecast promised a ninety percent chance of rain so I decided to stay put in the little town, spending on food the money I was saving on accommodation.

At Honbetsu Koen Park there were a few other frugal campers, all of them Japanese. There was a group of five in a large tent with a camper parked nearby, stocked up with boxes of drinks and food; a young couple with a little child, a motorbiker and Shinji, whom I got to know a little. He was in his sixties and had a precarious tent covered by another layer of blue tarpaulin, just in case it failed. He was walking around in a trekking outfit and told me he had come from Kobe. I asked him whether he had come to Hokkaido for the hiking.

"No, no...not me!" he said, waving his hand sideways in a typical Japanese gesture that means an unequivocal no.

"I come here to drink!" he told me, casually.

The campsite was set in the pristine grounds of a public park within a narrow valley, a couple of kilometres out of town.

With hardly anything around I asked where he was going to indulge in his pastime.

"Oh...I just go to town and buy it at the supermarket!" he said laughing.

The whole thing sounded to me like one of life's little tragedies. Few things would sadden me more than spending a holiday alone in a tent for the sake of consuming alcohol. But for Shinji, it seemed a perfectly natural thing to do. He had come all the way from Kobe to this campground in order to get tipsy, and told me he had done so for the last fifteen years of his life. Once mid September comes, he rides his small motorbike two hundred kilometres to reach the port of Tsuruga on the Japan Sea and boards an overnight ferry to Tomakomai in southern Hokkaido before riding all the way to Honbetsu campsite. If the purpose was solely to get stoned, with not much interest in sightseeing, I was about to ask why he didn't choose a location closer to home, but it would have been insensitive. With over a decade of experience visiting a small town that could be thoroughly explored in a single day, he knew everything that was free of charge. He didn't hesitate when I asked where I could charge my gadgets and spare batteries.

"Just go to Kirara Laundry Paradise inside Fukuhara supermarket."
"I go myself each morning to charge my phone," he said.

"It's in the far corner."
"They have comfortable chairs with tables, lots of plugs and free wifi."

"Don't I need to use the laundromat?" I asked him.

"Nah...nobody will know about it." he replied.

    He seemed to be on a rather tight budget and was not as knowledgeable about local restaurants. His food, like the booze, came straight from the shelves of Fukuhara supermarket. His motorbike was also interesting. I had already noticed a few people using that model for travelling around Hokkaido. It was a Honda Super Cub, a tiny but venerated motorcycle that for decades has been used by postmen in order to deliver mail all over Japan. Being Italian, its rounded shapes and old fashioned style reminded me of a Vespa, and among the Japanese it seemed to have a similar iconic following. Shinji was obviously extremely fond of it.

"It's indestructible!" he claimed.

"Nothing ever goes wrong with it...if made in Japan.", he was quick to add.

He told me how Honda, in order to save costs and cut corners, had made a short-lived attempt to shift production to China. Incredibly, Super Cubs started leaving people stranded with technical issues, infuriating postmen all over the country. There was an insurrection against Honda, which was forced to return production to Japan with lots of bows and copious apologies. Since then things had once more been fine and dandy, Shinji said, and the bike was as reliable as before.

The ninety percent chance of rain turned out to be closer to one hundred and I had made a good choice to stay put and make the sleepy village of Honbetsu home for an extra day. The morning started dry, letting me visit the extensive park around the campsite, manicured to perfection by dozens of talented gardeners. I thanked them for keeping things so tidy and for the free campsite. After a quick visit to the local shrine up the hill to pray for some sunshine it was time to indulge in some more good pork steaks at a recommended restaurant. While the husband was busy cooking just behind the counter, the wife stared at this rather odd customer who had just walked in wearing a bright orange poncho and holding a folded bike in one hand. We chatted a while about nearby places I should visit and food that was not to be missed, and I was pleased to have come at the start of October when she told me that Honbetsu gets temperatures as low as minus thirty in winter. I later spent some time warming up while watching the rain from a window table in the town's tourist office. Even this had been recommended by savvy Shinji who had warned me that sitting at a table for a long while was not exactly free but could be enjoyed for as long as I wanted by simply buying a cheap cup of coffee! Rain kept pouring down the whole afternoon, so I took cover under my poncho to make it back relatively dry to the campsite. As I arrived, Shinji was peeping through a slit of tarpaulin. He said hello and waved at me while holding in his other hand a silver can of Asahi. Despite the dreadful weather, he seemed pretty upbeat and happy.

It rained heavily into the night, but as expected it had all cleared by the time I woke up. I headed back to the launderette in order to dry the sleeping bag and spare clothes, which were a little damp from such a wet day. Not surprisingly, Shinji was already there; he had made sure to be there by seven o'clock, the opening time. He was also drying some of his stuff while chatting to the cleaning lady, whom he knew quite well after fifteen years of regular summer visits. We chatted some more among the spinning dryers. Before he took up drinking and a more sedentary style of holiday at Honbetsu campsite, he had been more adventurous and had travelled extensively around Hokkaido with his trusted Honda motorbike. He was most helpful with recommendations about hot springs and campsites that I should visit as I continued my ride. I couldn't decide between Lake Onneto and Lake Akan as a final destination for the day, but it was Shinji's knowledge that put an end to my dithering. Onneto he recommended and Onneto it was going to be. He said that nature, the campsite, and a nearby *onsen* were much better and much cheaper than at Akan, where most tourists tended to spend their time. So, after the town of Osharo I turned right following the road leading to Akan Mashu National Park. For about forty kilometres I hardly met any cars, but I managed to at least find a tiny café where Chica, who was behind the counter, was intrigued by my weird bicycle. I mentioned having recently visited Colombia, and my adventures on a bicycle were a sweet reminder of a solitary journey she had taken years earlier, a journey that was to this day the best time she had had in her life. She had backpacked for six months around Ecuador, Peru, Bolivia and Colombia. I opened up my tent to let it dry in the sun and, with some good coffee and a local ice cream, we shared our experiences and memories of common places we had visited in South America. An hour had hardly passed after leaving her café, nostalgically named El Camino. I continued up the mountains when dark clouds gathered around me and a mighty downpour started, with torrential rain. Luck had it that it started just as I was passing a small shrine with a wooden shed, whose roof practically saved me from drowning. With a strong wind, conditions changed within thirty minutes and a warm sun emerged to heat the asphalt, transforming water puddles into puffed up clouds of steam that soon disappeared. Along the road I counted about ten cars per hour and, with the eerie silence, the dark forests on either side reminded me that I was in bear country.

I started singing out loud some of the town jingles that were still roaming around in my head in an effort to announce myself and avoid any tragic encounters. I took a turn onto an even narrower and darker road leading to Onneto, which made me sing even louder. It was a little steeper than Shinji had told me, but I am sure it felt easier on his motorbike. As I wearily reached the top of the hill, I smelt the sulphur and saw the first spouts of steaming water rising from the river. I knew I had reached Nonoka Onsen and it couldn't have come at a better time. I enjoyed an hour of soaking, resting my tired legs in an outdoor pool as the sun slowly disappeared behind a hill thick with tall pine trees. It felt like bliss while it lasted. From there I knew it was just a short ride to Onneto lake with its two towering volcanic mountains and a few more minutes in order to reach the campsite. I reached it just before dusk. There were only five tents, and a stunning deer that was grazing the grass, completely ignoring me as I pitched my tent a few metres away.

- Lake Onneto, JAPAN -

It was an icy night at the forest campsite. I wore long-johns, trousers, my woollen hat, four top layers and a down jacket as if ready to go out on a winter night, but instead hid tightly down my sleeping bag. The Japanese are pretty sensitive to cold temperatures and by the morning there was plenty of coughing and sneezing going on around me.

The wise man of Chitose had seen it all clearly. Please be careful, he had told me, minutes before experiencing the first broken bicycle chain in my entire life. Perhaps I hadn't taken his advice seriously enough: maybe due to carelessness, my ultralight, ultra-fragile and ultra expensive camping mattress developed a minuscule leak. As I was lying on it, during the night it slowly deflated and woke me up with a sore, cold back. I inflated it again, thinking I might have not sealed the valve, but after three hours I was back on hard soil, which compounded the intrinsic difficulties of properly resting at a campsite. The mattress came with repair patches, but the hole turned out to be so tiny that even the man from Chitose would have found it hard to find. A large basin of water was needed to immerse it in. I pondered breaking rule thirty seven of hot springs etiquette, which warns against bringing an inflatable mattress inside the hot baths, but I knew it would be risky; it would irreparably damage the reputation of us foreigners if someone was to find me, which given the bright yellow of the mattress was extremely likely.

Out of the five people I spoke with yesterday, four ended their conversation with a *ki o tsukete* and the fifth was so elderly that I thought I should say it first. Compared to other countries worldwide, Japan's crime is practically non-existent. Something as trivial as pickpocketing happens so rarely that it makes it to the evening news. To compensate, every now and then something un-imaginable and ghastly happens, but that's about it and it soon gets forgotten, everyone quickly returning to their orderly lives. Nowhere else can you be sure to find your wallet that slipped out of your pocket, complete with all the money down to the last penny. No one ever said 'please be careful' in the crime-infested streets of the large cities of Colombia, where all kinds of calamities indeed happen. Judging Japan by these constant reminders and warnings, you'd think you had landed in a particularly dangerous country.

I passed by lake Akan and, after climbing five hundred metres, coasted downhill all the way to the town of Teshikaga where I had planned to spend the night at yet another campsite. Once back on the plains the landscape was transformed, with extensive hilly pastures as green as green can be, massive specimens of Holstein Friesian cows and a pungent smell of shit reminiscent of rural Bavaria. The campsite itself was set on a farm. The elegant wooden hut that functioned as the reception building was shut, and there was a paper notice written in

Japanese. I needed some help to decipher it and attracted the attention of an elderly man in a track suit and trainers who had been walking energetically backwards for the last ten minutes. He was most kind, stopped reversing and called the owner, who said he would be coming shortly and that in the meantime I could pick any place. Given that the Japanese are health freaks and champions of longevity, I thought I should research this backwards walking on the internet. I discovered that walking backwards is indeed a thing! Provided one does not mind looking a little odd, and avoids injuries, it apparently brings many benefits ranging from improved mobility to better cognition. The highlight of the evening was a large bowl of ramen with a side dish of fried dumplings, after which I headed to the local *onsen* for an unmissable dip. There I met with a group of cyclists who were attending a cycling event the next day. They were downbeat about the weather, most of them sure that it would be raining and stormy. I prepared a plan B which focused less on distance, more on having a good time and was kept in reserve for when the weather turned stroppy; it consisted of hopping from hot spring to hot spring, fairly easy to arrange around here.

However, whoever up there is in charge of the weather worked some kind of miracle, and I have to be deeply grateful. The naked cyclists at the *onsen* had been far too pessimistic. It did look dreadful to start with, but it slowly improved as soon as I began the ascent towards Mashu lake. As I reached the top some clouds were still scudding around but the sunshine pierced through them just at the right time, allowing me a clear view of the volcanic lake and Kamuinupuri mountain right behind it. As I started my descent down the other side I spotted four eagles hovering in circles just above me, scanning the ground for prey. One of them suddenly dived not too far ahead of me, picking up what was left of a mouse that had been squashed flat under the tyres of a car. Before reaching Kawayu Onsen I was in for a surprise. To my left was Iozan mountain from whose banks spurted clouds of sulphur that rose up in spirals and smelt like spent matches.

By now I knew that I should let my love for the Japanese spas determine my cycling distances and that the short time I was so fortunate to spend here should not be wasted or taken for granted. I luxuriated in them, happy to let them mess up my original plans. A daily visit to the local hot spring, if one is lucky to live near one, is amongst the favourite Japanese rituals. People of all ages come at the end of a long day to soak away their stress and forget all their worries by sitting motionless in piping hot mineral waters, often with a white towel folded on top of their heads. They are ideal places to strike up a conversation with a stranger and places where status and achievements are left behind and forgotten. Inside the pools, everyone is stark naked, taken back to that primordial nature that makes us all the same. In Kawayu Onsen I broke rule number nine: "Do Not Do Your Laundry In The Washing Room". It was only a minor infraction that went completely unnoticed as all I washed was a pair of grey underpants. The day could not have been better.. Once again it was time to be grateful and get some rest in my tent pitched by the shores of Kusharo lake.

The start of the day was promising, with a sun rising on a cloudless sky as I got ready to tackle a ten kilometre climb to the top of Bihoro pass. Gradients were steady and manageable even with the luggage I carried. I made steady progress through a thick canopy of birch, oak and maple trees which, had it been a month later, would have lit up the ridge slopes with the warm hues of autumn. A few kilometres short of the top, the tall trees vanished leaving a vegetation of low bushes and green grass and revealing picture perfect views of lake Kusharo down below. I stopped at the top and sat on a flat rock to take it all in from the best vantage point money could buy. The road continued down the other side, winding its way to the north coast.

There were more columns of military jeeps and trucks pulling long trailers, carrying bulky artillery that reminded me of far off wars that jarred with the palpable tranquillity of Hokkaido's landscape. I began to spot the first glimpses of water and the faint shapes of Russia's Kuril Islands just a stone's throw away. I had been exploring the interior of the island, crossing mountains and coasting lakes, but I could now smell the unmistakable briny smell of the sea. The mountain slopes descended to the plains, where Hokkaido's farmers, on their tractors and ploughs, were hard at work to feed Japan. At a T-junction I came across the quaint wooden structure of Mokoto station, where just a single railway track stood between me and the Okhotsk Sea. To reach the town of Shari I followed the coast along a straight, flat road for thirty kilometres, the tedium being relieved by a constant westerly tailwind. Without any chance to relax at an *onsen,* I covered just short of a hundred kilometres that day, and this turned out to be the longest stage of the entire trip. After many nights of camping, and futile attempts to sleep on a mattress that was still leaking, I looked forward to a proper bed. I had booked a room at Both Hostel, a brand new property that turned out to be one of the best hostels I have ever stayed in (and I have by now stayed in quite a few).

As a last treat, I had decided to visit Shiretoko National Park, a UNESCO world heritage site that prides itself as the home of the largest population of brown bears in Japan. I thought I should brush up my knowledge on bear scat, long forgotten since I did some research prior to touring Alberta and British Columbia. I browsed multiple images on the internet and read detailed explanations on how they differ between grizzlies, brown and black bears, but to me they all looked pretty much the same. A bit of a waste of time really, like the useless bell I was carrying. I read how in winter, although they do not hibernate, they enter a lighter state of sleep called torpor. Luck had it that October was exactly the month when they actively searched for prey in order to fatten up and survive the harsh winter.

Following the coastal road to Utoro I had to put up with a series of downpours and much fresher temperatures. I stopped in the town to warm up with a cup of coffee and to gather some food, not unlike what bears do, and then started the climb up to Shiretoko pass that was completely hidden by a veil of leaden clouds. Halfway, I took a short break at the National Park Office where a Japanese man and his wife approached me; they said they had already seen me a few times over the past few days, while driving around the roads of Hokkaido, and they had apparently stayed at Onneto campsite on the same night I had been there. They were living in the beautiful town of Kamakura on the outskirts of Tokyo and what most excited them was that they also owned a Brompton, although they had never imagined travelling on one. I continued a few miles further along the road when a car hooted and then stopped, waiting for me to catch up. A cheerful lady stretched her arm out of the passenger window to hand me a set of three bells:

"It's dangerous around here!" she said, failing to reassure me.
"You'll need these more than we do..."
I thanked her loudly for her generosity while keeping quiet about the fact that she had just scared me more.

I moved on courageously, now with four clinking bells and keeping up a loud medley of all the Beatles songs I could remember. Incredibly, despite the angry looking sky, not a drop of rain fell on me. Rather it was the gusts of wind that got me a little worried; they had been strong all the way up but picked up pace as I was about to summit the pass, with gusts that pushed me up without the need to keep pedalling, but making it a challenge to keep balance even when standing. It felt freezing cold up there in the wind. I stopped only briefly and chatted with a young Japanese motorcyclist who was on an inaugural trip with his brand new sporty bike. We debated how safe it would be to continue, but we also knew that despite the wind it was certainly not safe to stay where we were. I descended the mountain and after a few bends conditions got much calmer until I reached Kuma No

Yu (which could be translated into English as Bears Hot Spa). I had long planned stopping there and it had been mentioned several times along the way. It was very easy to miss but at a certain point I noticed a few cars parked to the side of the road; an elderly man who was there confirmed it was nearby and that I would find it by walking along a path and crossing a narrow bridge. I walked down a series of steps before reaching a flimsy wooden shack where, in a one awful moment, I squandered all the good deeds I had done to be a well mannered foreigner in Japan. I had made an effort to be polite at all times, had smiled at people I encountered and even greeted some with a tentative bow when it all went pear-shaped. And now, for the second time in my life, I found myself breaking rule number one of *onsen* etiquette:

"DO NOT WALK INTO THE LADIES POOLS"

- Kuma No Yu, JAPAN -

The first time it happened to me was over a decade ago. Most if not all public *onsen* have separate male and female areas whose entrances are usually marked by a pink and a blue curtain with large white printed characters indicating which one is which. Perhaps to be fair and equal, I have since realised that they usually swap the two areas around, for example having males on one side on even days and the opposite side on odd days. In the outskirts of Tokyo I paid a couple of visits to an *onsen,* both times on an odd day. The third time around I was not so lucky. I walked confidently through the same door I had used the previous times, finding myself face to face with a couple of elderly and stark naked ladies who were about to get changed; even more embarrassing, given their age, was the fact that it took me some time to become aware of what I had done. They didn't seem to mind my presence in the least and kept drying themselves as if nothing had happened. As for me, I made a hasty exit, bright red in the face.

Back at Kuma No Yu things worked out differently. As I arrived, I saw a group of men bathing in an outdoor pool to the side. I leaned my bike against the hut and, eager to soak my tired bones and muscles, pushed open a door to the side assuming it must be the changing room. Rule number one had once again been broken, this time with an eloquent and much younger lady who obviously minded my presence! At lightning speed she covered herself in a towel while crouching and began screaming and pointing her finger to make it absolutely clear that men should go to the other side. I bowed and apologised before moving next door where five local men from the town of Rausu stared at me as if an alien had just landed; they probably realised what had happened and the reason for all the commotion and shouting which had disturbed their peaceful place. I had started off on the wrong foot and couldn't help feel that they didn't particularly like me. I assume they were regulars, coming daily from the village down below, and perhaps keen to keep their own thermal paradise a secret. I undressed in the correct cabin, and got ready to join them in the small natural pool immersed in the woods by the side of a brook. One of them was particularly unfriendly. Before I had reached the side of the pool he started mumbling instructions, bossing me around as if he had recently retired from an illustrious career as a Sergeant Major in the army. I didn't understand half of what he was telling me, but he obviously had a talent for expressing things forcefully and I got the jist of it. Everything had to be done following a precise sequence and in the correct place.

"Go back to the shed and take a bucket!" he first told me.

It would have been pointless arguing.
I returned armed with a little bucket and was about to collect some pool water to douse it over my body to rinse it when he stopped me there and then.

"Not here!"
"Go over there to rinse." he said, again forcefully, while pointing me to a tap that was along a path to the side.

I returned to the pool, rinsed and with an empty bucket, awaiting orders, but he kept silent.

Finally, time to relax and to soak.

"No!" he bellowed as I put down the bucket to one side ready to enter the pool.

I wondered what I had done wrong this time.

"You must fill it with water first or it'll fly away."

The tone was excessive but there was wisdom in what he said and it was indeed very windy. I dipped my toes in the water and withdrew them immediately. I remembered that Shinji had mentioned that this *onsen* was notorious for the hot temperature of its water. I couldn't believe it. In front of me were five men in their sixties and seventies, perfectly at ease, fully immersed in a pool where one could cook some perfectly set boiled eggs. It was piping hot and they all laughed at me. A kinder man gestured that I should first get adjusted to the shock by gently pouring water over my body from the outside. Once more the bucket came in handy. I scooped some water and poured it over my head.

"No...!" said by now we know who.

Pouring water over one's hair was not a done thing and he gestured I should pour it from my shoulders down instead.

After about ten minutes of this water basting, the body somehow adjusted and resigned itself to being steamed: I took a plunge in the cauldron and experienced how there can be pleasure in pain. I took to it, soaking several times like a native. The initial hostility changed and I felt accepted. When I mentioned where I was originally from, Sergeant Major bellowed a '*Mussolini!*', not surprisingly, the only Italian word he had ever learnt.

Despite the stressful start I thoroughly enjoyed my visit to Kuma No Yu and got back on the bike feeling rejuvenated, with the skin a medium-rare purple colour that lasted well into the evening. I had been warned that the nearby campsite might be closed, and so it was. I was told in Rausu that this year they had closed it earlier on safety grounds, due to the unusual quantity of bears. I searched for an alternative place to stay. I was told there might be rooms at Washi No Yado just outside the village. When I reached it I found a series of prefabricated cabins placed along the bank of a small stream, not unlike those large containers that are seen on cargo ships. What was more unusual though was that at each window I noticed a series of cameras mounted on tripods and pointing to the river. Behind each one there was a photographer who, given the extraordinarily large zooms, must have been waiting for a particularly small insect. It did not seem a particularly suitable place for cyclists but I entered the container that functioned as a dining room as well as reception area and asked whether I could stay.

"Do you have a reservation?", asked the lady behind the counter.

"No…"

"I am afraid we are full…" she said, adding that usually the place is fully booked half a year in advance!

I had inadvertently walked into a world-renowned bird sanctuary, one of the only two places where photographers can hope to see one of the few remaining fishing owls worldwide. According to the latest count there are barely two hundred left, all to be found in this area of Hokkaido. Photographers had flocked from all over Japan, but there were also two from Hong Kong and a group of six from Thailand. They were all waiting for the elusive bird to feed on fish at night, illuminated by a strategically positioned set of spotlights. As for me, it was getting too late to find anywhere else and as I was about to leave I mentioned I had a tent and that I would pitch it in a park nearby.

"Don't do that!" said the lady, "there's plenty of bears around here at night."

She was worried enough about me to make a phone call to her husband, no doubt a world authority on fishing owls, before offering me a second floor room in their house. I wished all the photographers the best of luck for the night and looked forward to getting some rest on a futon mattress.

I woke up during the night and thought I should check out how the photographers were doing. It was one in the morning. Five of them were in the dining room, which besides having a good series of windows overlooking the river had also a brewing machine with complimentary coffee to keep them all alert and awake. The Japanese man from Sapporo, who had shown me his collection of stunning wildlife pictures as I arrived, silently pointed at a barren tree with a few branches; a perfectly still silhouette of a fishing owl was perched there. Nothing was guaranteed, despite the steep prices for a night in a container, so most photographers were happy it had at least showed up, but the Thai lot were growing impatient. The bird was not exactly where the light was shining, on a rockery arranged in the middle of the brook, but rather in a shaded corner where it could hardly be seen or photographed. The coffee kept flowing; I heard it had been sitting there motionless for the last three hours, without the slightest interest in showing itself in all its beauty, let alone catching any fish. In the meantime I was shown a few pictures from previous years and, with binoculars that were set up on top of a counter, I could see the shapes of its grey feathers and its yellow eyes piercing through the dark of the night. A stunning bird it was, but also one that tested patience.

Another trip was drawing to a close, with the other half of the Shiretoko loop still awaiting me. I was happy it was only on the last day, in a Park Office, that I learnt how bears can run at a speed of fifty kilometres per hour when chasing, which is about as fast as my loaded bicycle can descend the steepest hill. I first followed the coastline facing Kunashir, the closest of the Russian Kuril Islands. Before reaching the town of Shibetsu I found myself once again in mountainous terrain and returned to singing some of my favourite Beatles' tunes. After summiting the final pass it was downhill and back to the town of Shari. Forests once again disappeared, replaced by crops of sugar beet and wheat. For the second time on my trip I was treated to the sight of two red-crowned cranes feeding in a field of tall grass before taking off in the most majestic of flights.

Shinji had been right after all - not about the alcohol consumption, but that after experiencing this journey, returning back to Hokkaido every summer for fifteen years did not sound such a bad idea. The last conversation in Hokkaido was with a seventy year old man from Singapore called Yang, an encounter that was timely and most appropriate. We met at the bus station. I was on my way to the airport for a journey back to the routines of regular life while he was waiting for a short bus ride to the city of Abashiri, continuing a long series of uninterrupted travels that had kept him busy and cheerful for the last thirty years of his life. I told him about my future plan to do something similar and also mentioned my fears and worries.

"Do you have a wife, or kids?" he asked. No, I replied.
"Old parents to look after? A mortgage to pay"? No and no.

"Same here." he said with a smile on his face.

"Why wait another year?"

I have since renamed him the 'Messenger of Shari'.

Printed in Great Britain
by Amazon